Close Up and Personal

Close Up and Personal

Catherine Deneuve

Translated by Polly McLean

ORION

First published in France in 2004 under the title
A L'Ombre de Moi-Même by Editions Stock

First published in Great Britain in 2005
by Orion Books, a division of
the Orion Publishing Group Ltd
Orion House
5 Upper Saint Martin's Lane
London
WC2H 9EA

A CIP catalogue record for this book is available
from the British Library

ISBN 0 75286 951 5

Typeset, printed and bound in Great Britain by
Butler and Tanner Ltd, Frome and London

www.orionbooks.co.uk

CONTENTS

Let me warn you that these are mere jottings, personal records of the shootings of films, chronicles of my doubts. Almost all were written outside France, and some a long time ago. Solitary, elated, discouraged, critical. Raw. A little remorse, perhaps, but no regrets.

Catherine Deneuve

Dancer in the Dark

1999

Director: Lars von Trier

Screenplay: Lars von Trier

Cast: Björk (Selma), Catherine Deneuve
(Kathy), David Morse (Bill), Peter
Stormare (Jeff), Jean-Marc Barr
(Norman)

Director of photography: Robby Müller

Costume designer: Manon Rasmussen

Music: Björk

Release date: 2000

May 1999
To Copenhagen. Gazing at fields of rape through the plane window; they're like a Poliakoff painting, jagged. Very sore throat, feverish. It's raining when I arrive at the hotel, top floor, wooden balcony, everyone will pass my windows on the way to the neighbouring rooms! Meeting with Lars at his place, in his little log cabin at the end of the garden. We're meant to do a read-through with Björk, but she doesn't come, she's in town feeling unwell; her agent calls from London to say that she won't be able to make it. We talk a little, I feel that it's hard to explain or analyse what 'motivates' him, leave pretty early and go back to the hotel for the rest of the day. Horrible weather, big fit of the blues.

The next day. To the studio for the official tour of the set. Gorgeous brick military buildings twenty minutes out of town, converted into studios, offices, a canteen, new sets being built, and Lars's office right at the very end, buried, a bit like a bunker. With piles of empty ammunition boxes in the doorway! They really should clear away the huge mound of earth blocking his window.

Later. More set-building, but basic – all our energy must go into the film. Read-through with Björk who arrives wrapped up like an Eskimo, in striped tights and clogs, a bit wild and shy, but fairly relaxed with this informal read-through. Jean-Marc Barr has been flown in from Paris for the day, he doesn't ask anything in particular. Lars seems more or less happy. Nothing on the costumes, and me sick with flu, no reason to stay, so I leave pretty quickly, relieved almost and a little

3

anxious, unsure of the solidity of all this. Have I already signed?

Return to Copenhagen to rehearse the musical scene in the factory, and for costume fittings and screen tests. On the time sheet everything is clear and precise; a huge number of people must work in this studio. Hammers banging all over the place, but things are actually pretty vague and disordered. It'll take me a while to realise this is his way of doing things. The project is unwieldy; preparations are running late and he has this enormous need to discover, and especially to retain, a certain 'freshness' for the shoot. Almost all the period clothing comes from Seattle in the US. The prospect of not having to be 'well turned out' is quite appealing. But the tailoring, fabric and colours are of poor quality. What will I think of all this in two months' time?

Dinner with Lars and the producer at a restaurant. He doesn't stay for the whole meal, too long; until recently, he was physically unable to be in a restaurant. Another time we have dinner with Björk. We drink wine, she's cheerful, shy, available. I watch Lars. She's made him wait a long time, and occasionally I feel resentment building in him. I think that basically everything will be very professional because Lars knows what he wants, everyone will follow his lead, which must be a burden for him sometimes. This is a big production for these guys, probably the first. Filming has been postponed twice, I'll finally start on 1 June. I'm leaving for Gothenburg in Sweden. I know they've already shot the scene with the moving train and the 100 cameras, all hidden, of course, because Lars films 360 degrees. The hours were horrendous, they went over schedule and everything. Björk got exhausted, and they had to stop for a couple of days. She and I are due to start the bus scene. There's a bit of a row, Lars gives his

explanation and then decides to film the 'rehearsal' –
something he'll do repeatedly as we go on. Lars films
everywhere and everything. He's delighted because he
wants this kind of material to lighten up the scripted
aspect of the scenes. He goes so far as to say that the
script has no importance. It's the tone, the aliveness of
our relationship that he wants, which I can understand.

Björk asks me if film shoots are always like this! She
just says 'OK', drops her eyes and throws herself into it.
I was surprised when right on the first read-through,
alone in his office with the coach, he made us improvise.
I told her that this was a first for me too, but she wasn't
worried. She radiates such incredible sincerity and
feeling, inextinguishable, like the little white horse in that
song by Brassens.

That day we did some pick-ups for the bus scene and
in the afternoon the scene in the jewellery shop where I
have to be silently disapproving. He told me, rightly, that
I should be looking at Björk and not at the jeweller
standing by the camera, as if I wanted to make an exhib-
ition of my distress. I trust him completely. We spend
almost three hours on the scene, all of it unrehearsed,
and by the end I'm doing almost exactly the opposite of
what was in the script. Improvising in English is hard;
the coach takes me up on the way I say 'no' questioningly,
as we do in French. Björk rolls her 'r's like the Scots. I
saw her arriving at her trailer this morning, she doesn't
wear make-up, she just screws her hair into little coils
and clips them while she's chatting, without so much as
a glance in the mirror. She never wanted to have her hair
cut in the style of the period, as she perhaps should have
done, so she just twists it back as best she can.

Early dinner at the hotel, with Lars, merry, drinking
beer and aquavit. We eat at 7.30 because we get up early

and need our sleep. Of course, I sleep very badly, the bed is wedged into an alcove, the curtains aren't lined, and I need total darkness. I've picked some wild blue lupins; the seasons here in Sweden come a month later than in France, and in their old champagne bucket, they really add cheer to my room.

Day in Gothenburg. Chilly and bright. It's the end of the student year, and the girls and boys are partying in their cars as if they're on carnival floats, singing and shouting and wearing white caps. The light is stunning, there's no pollution and lots of the adorable neat little wooden houses are painted this wonderful soft reddish-ochre colour, so dark it's almost black. I discover it contains a lot of iron oxide and is found only around here. The name of the earth is *falnrödfarg*. Must get some to paint my sheep-hut. As you go north, the countryside becomes even more beautiful, hilly, with almost no cars, no trains, nothing, like in the olden days, very green – it rains almost every day – and then these huge lakes. When we arrive, I walk to the lake despite the light rain and the two and a half-hour drive. It's a bit like Ireland. The hotel is charming – no phones in the rooms, quite spacious and completely empty, feels like being in the mountains. I'll only be shooting here for a day. There'll be no rehearsals. There are quite a few of us. Selma, her son, Jeff, Bill and his wife, and me. The scene unfolds as we improvise more and more, a spontaneous, modest party for the gift of the bicycle to the child. I think in the end it lasted nearly twenty minutes. Lars is delighted, he says so again in Copenhagen. How I'd love to recapture this energy, this simultaneous concentration and abandonment, in Copenhagen.

Return to Copenhagen for three days of rehearsals. Choreographing the court scene. There are a lot of us.

On the second day, we have to focus hard because the moves are precise, but the space is very tight and I don't have much to do; don't feel very involved. Too long for too little, and what's more, it'll be a month till we shoot. Back to Paris.

Sunday 20 June

Return for rehearsals in the factory. I've forgotten a lot but the body remembers and is quick to gets its bearings. My part isn't especially hard, but the dance sequence is precise and they're using professional dancers; the gap mustn't show too much. The first time, I got it quickly and was quite proud of myself. Not so today. I'm aware that we have to get everything up to scratch, and keep it so for the shoot. A hundred cameras. Just for fun I try to spot them, they're well hidden so they can get all the angles, because Lars only wants to shoot two or three takes, with no pick-up. According to him something crucial gets lost in retakes. He's been forced to do retakes twice by Björk. She couldn't bring herself to knock Bill out before pulling the trigger, or to slap her son. I was watching, it was impossible, they ended up doing that classic trick where the head follows the movement of the slap, but I doubt he'll keep that take. Her son is played by a young Serb, a boxer in the making, sensitive and aggressive. The machines are dirty and greasy. I work levers, stamping sink rims; the machines are chunky and noisy and old, from the 1950s I suppose.

The music Björk has written for the film is amazing. I can't wait to see the rushes, even though it will only be on a TV monitor as the footage will get blown up for the cinema later. I know that in Sweden they've seen a few seconds of film shot with the 100 cameras; apparently it looks fantastic, the colours are extraordinary, and the enlargement process really softens the whole thing. A bit like old films, as Lars says. He even shot Björk in the river with an underwater camera.

Return to The Admiral Hotel. I like this top-floor room overlooking the harbour, with its three windows and beautiful light. I can watch the liners going out and the fishing boats coming in. I realised early on that there was no point in asking Lars to explain my character further, because I don't have many scenes. Trying to create a character so different from me. I tell myself that Kathy will be what I make of her, what I am able to do through improvisation. It's a bit like a competition: I know the start but not the finish. Björk, of course, will be omnipresent, but the other characters will be what we make of them. I know he'll keep what seems to him true and alive. It's an exciting process.

Monday 21 June
Dress rehearsal in the factory. Almost everything forgotten since last month, the dancers say it's the same for them, but they get it back much quicker. I don't have the energy I had then, must go to bed earlier – the days are long and the rhythm disjointed.

Second day. Harder going, more of a struggle, no feeling of progress. I sense Björk's distress at Lars's comment this morning about 'generosity' – 'complicity' would have been strong enough. I try to resolve the misunderstanding, but I can see she's unhappy. Before leaving at about three, I give her a hug. She is weary and distraught, and this evening it's me who's sad.

Wednesday 23 June
Filming in the factory. Luckily, it's not a hot day; I'm out of breath at the end of each take. The whole scene is shot

in one go. I hope that with the 100 cameras he'll be able to retain only the best. Will he have enough wide shots?

Thursday 24 June

Machines, everybody working, more shots with the dancers. An unbelievable racket, you have to shout to make yourself heard. Still improvising, but Lars knows what he's doing, never losing sight of the truth of his characters. Because of the lenses his camera is very heavy, fifteen kilos (thirty-three pounds) maybe, and with takes sometimes lasting thirty or forty minutes it's really tough going, even with his support belt. I see him in the mornings when he's rehearsing, taking off his t-shirt to pull on the harness, his torso frail and pale like the baby doll's I had as a child. His strength is elsewhere, but what stamina! He's very good fun.

Go to the seaside Louisiana Museum. A serious collection, and such beautiful sculptures in the garden overlooking the sea – an impressive and welcoming place. I love the atmosphere in the cafés and restaurants, always candlelit even at lunchtime, beautiful lighting. They're used to living indoors because the days are so short here. The city is very pretty, gorgeous buildings, warehouses converted into housing, like my hotel, The Admiral.

Monday 28 June

We'll soon be finished with this set, and my ears will be grateful. But what a factory! All the machines function, and in each scene, wherever it is, everyone has something to do, including the dancers and the technicians. A veritable beehive. I'm furious with myself for the scene in the factory where I have to get angry. Mediocre, not fluent enough with the script. Why do I never get it exactly right? Impossible to learn my lines perfectly. Laziness?

Fear of sounding mechanical? I often think of André Téchiné and that awful time when we were in Lyon filming *Thieves*; he was both wrong and right, but I was so hurt.

It's hard to prepare yourself with Lars; you're hanging around all the time but have to be ready to start at a moment's notice, without preparing anything. It's osmosis, you have to follow his lead. Interactive. Anyway, not very proud today. I think he's more or less satisfied, I talk to him before lunch, he tells me that in any case he'll keep the bare essentials, some of the dialogues weren't that great, a bit too laboured. It's probably the English translation. That's why he's so keen for us to get away from the script and improvise.

I like this room at The Admiral, the beams, the simplicity of the furniture, the view of the port, the *Crown of Scandinavia* leaving every evening for Sweden. And the space – so often hotel rooms are suffocating, cluttered with useless furniture to make you feel 'at home'. My candle, pretty engraved vases, a little cushion and some flowers. Perfect.

Return from Paris on 5 July. Lars is there, at the airport, waiting for Vibeke, the producer. He hasn't been filming, he's devastated about the aggression and conflict, he's smashed up a television set. Björk called him a coward, and last week, a tyrant, and he hasn't been shooting today. Vibeke is rushing back from Italy. Summit at Björk's place tonight around eleven. He tells me things are starting to resolve themselves and she'll film tomorrow.

Monday 12 July

At the studio for eight o'clock. Preparation, and then the news that she won't be coming. She wants the final cut

on the musical numbers. Her English agent has told her
not to come to the studio until he's negotiated; I suppose
he doesn't know that the contract doesn't allow that.
What thoughtlessness about the production – there are
still thirty-five dancers here, how dare they? Imagine if
I'd called my agent Bertrand with that request at six
o'clock this morning. She's used to being the centre of
everything and wants to control it all. At around eleven,
we go to the studio café and consider every option. But
first the lawyers must be consulted about her rights over
the music. Who owns what, whether she continues with
the shoot or not? A few hours later, Lars turns up, agitated, looking for a solution. He needed at least eight
more days to ensure the near completion of the film,
which is both a little and a lot; we thought we'd have
another three weeks. He's worried, hurt, sickened and
finally furious. We even contemplate using a stand-in and
some technical fiddling for the court scene. I suggest that
since it's possible to combine actors and animations to
make films like *Roger Rabbit*, perhaps he could overlay
the huge amount of material he must already have with
voice-overs. All the songs have already been recorded.
Well, we're all pretty angry and desperate for a solution.

Vibeke seems very worried, but not particularly vin-
dictive towards the agent. All this would be unthinkable
in a normal context, but with hindsight it seems that this
current situation has its roots in a conflict which had been
latent since the beginning. Her hesitation, her refusals,
then everyone's feeling of discouragement after this had
gone on for a year, her renunciation and, after all that,
final acceptance of the role, and the contract signed – but
given her personality, and habit of throwing herself into
all her projects, and genius for writing music ... power
struggles, of course, but also compromises, and many

positive achievements, up to a certain point. Her music is wonderful, so original, but she's had to make a lot of unhappy compromises for someone used to always working on her own.

Although I don't really feel like it, I offer to meet her in a café on my own, if that might help. The rest of us go our separate ways in the afternoon, linked by our mobiles. The director of her record company is on his way from London; he seems more rational. I hang around town, in cafés, talking on the phone, waiting, my state of mind darkening as the time passes, this is all crazy, absurd, and so sad. I had suggested to Vibeke that she explain the cost of a day, or even a half-day's shooting, thinking that this would make them realise the seriousness of the situation and the resources committed. Not a bit of it! Björk even asked how much it would cost to break the contract. Has she got the resources for that kind of indulgence? I wouldn't be so sure. Twelve million dollars is a lot of work.

A long discussion in the evening. Eventually, Lars agreed to go over to her place. He stayed until eleven, by which time it seems they'd reached an agreement. On what basis? I don't know. Even 'mutual agreement' has been rejected by them all – and I can see that it wouldn't be acceptable to a filmmaker like him. Restart tomorrow? Rehearsals in the morning and shooting in the afternoon.

Tuesday 13 July
I'm pretty discouraged, I don't care anymore. Björk turns up around eleven, which isn't unusual, but without a word of explanation or apology to me or anyone, not a single word. There's no point in expecting logical behaviour from her; you have to accept her as she is, wild and unique. I've lost my desire to understand, it's gone. I

know it'll never be like before, which is so unfortunate because it had seemed to me that the atmosphere, and general goodwill, and bonding around Lars were extraordinary. In fact, I think the problem might be that he's the heart of the film. I think it's hard for her to accept feeling, as she might put it, that she's living out the nightmare in *Rosemary's Baby*. Everyone so charming, warm, smiling, and she confronted with them, these 'monsters'. What can you say? Maybe almost all her entourage just give tacit approval to her decisions. Moods, longings, ruthless refusals . . . she's irrational and unmanageable. For me it's over – nothing will mend this fracture. Since Friday, Lars has seemed relieved.

Friday 16 July
The scene before the hanging has been filmed. Very tough. Lars still jumpy and agitated because of Björk. How is she going to react? Maybe she'll crack. He wants to take the least risk possible in case he can only shoot once, because you never know. He asked me to come an hour early to figure everything out, so that Björk can arrive and start shooting straight away, with no rehearsal, of course, as always, this scene's very tough for me also. I sense that he doesn't really want to think about it – he's got enough going on with the Icelandic management. As usual, I'm the good little soldier you can count on, so responsible, wanting everything to work out whatever happens – which is often to the good of the film. A long time after we filmed *Call Me Savage*, I remember Jean-Paul Rappeneau saying that he regretted having had to pay so much attention to Yves Montand, who was sometimes a source of tension, and in the process almost forgetting about me. It's the same here; Lars counts on me but doesn't have much time to devote. I don't cause

problems, and a director is a bit like a fireman, always attending to what's most urgent. It's a pretty sad state of affairs; I've almost finished and I haven't really immersed myself in the film, perhaps because there have been so many delays and changes of heart, and it's been a fast shoot with few scenes, more like sequences.

Lars was very worked up on the day we shot the hanging scene, and then we finished early. Not many shots, all long and following on from each other, the crew distraught, Lars smiling with fake cynicism – 'Good therapy, isn't it?' he commented to me. But he can breathe again now that this scene is shot, because no matter what happens at the end he'll be able to manage. Two more scenes in the visiting room and that'll be it for me. In the studio, in Copenhagen, he can finally really focus on her. It's Selma's story first and foremost; we're just support characters, which I hope in the end won't make for too unbalanced a film.

Two days in Sweden. A day's indoor filming – this scene absolutely has to be shot in Sweden. We even film the outdoor scene in the corridor – it was meant to be done in America, but Lars won't be there as he can't travel, and he probably wants to make sure it gets done just in case. There are still a few frustrations, despite the confidence of his assistant, an old film-school tutor of his. I don't stay for the party. Too much officialdom here in the studio. I'll sleep at the airport, my flight leaves at 7 a.m. I buy some more red-tinted earth, I love this Swedish soil, and the landscape. Last dinner with the boys, overlooking the water.

To Seattle via San Francisco; I'm bringing my friend Ursula as make-up artist. A fifteen-hour journey. I love this low-lying city on the water; it's so 1950s. The hotel is creepy, so I go and lose myself in the port. Only a few scenes, an outdoor one at Walla Walla, an hour's flight away but still in Washington State – vast farms in a giant landscape. There are traces of snow around the prison, and it's quite pretty – yet this is a high-security penitentiary with armed guards on the roof twenty-four hours a day. They've got walk-on parts, and over a picnic lunch spread on white tablecloths, they tell us how excited they are. Unsurprisingly, when they're on duty they aren't allowed to listen to music, or smoke, or anything, for the whole twelve-hour shift. So they're well paid. Caroline is going to visit the prison tomorrow, but I don't fancy it.

An outdoor dinner with the crew, around three big tables with candles and a bonfire – there's nothing but cottages around the house. We leave Walla Walla. They farm so strangely here, circular fields, as perfect as giant water lilies, brown or purple depending on the stage of the crop. I can't think of a rational reason for it, because the corners are lost. The irrigation is done from the centre like the hands of a clock.

Tomorrow we'll shoot in Arlington, in a main street, with vintage cars and the city just as it was, continuity shots, nothing to add or to take away to get the right era. Outside the cinema and the jeweller's. It's the last day of filming, conclusion of the same scene we shot on my first day of filming in Sweden.

I sit next to Björk at lunch. Bizarrely, she starts asking me about film shoots in general, still wanting to know if they're always like this. I'm pretty surprised; I know, because she's told me, that she's suffered a lot, and that Lars has constantly pushed her beyond her limits. Why didn't she ever say 'No', or 'That's enough'? I don't think of asking her this simple question, and then she doesn't come to the end-of-filming dinner that evening. So I'll never know – unless I spend Millennium Eve in Iceland at the end of this year. Perhaps she needed to tell me that in order to justify her refusals, and particularly the times she abandoned the shoot. She's very intelligent, I can't quite understand how she experienced such pressure and felt like she was going mad, pushed to extremes and losing her bearings. I know she got her way about being in on the editing of the song and dance numbers.

I haven't seen a single rush, a single photo, and it hasn't bothered me. I liked the experience, without making any true connections, apart from Caroline – but then they're northern Europeans. I was so unlike the character – how will she turn out? Lars is itching to edit. He'll take three days off, watch the eclipse in Jutland, and then tackle the editing. He gives the mountain of footage to three different editors, one of whom is French. He's waiting for Cannes, we're all determined – especially him – to meet at the Hotel du Cap in 2000.

East–West

1998

Director: Régis Wargnier

Screenplay: Régis Wargnier, Segueï Bodrov, Louis Gardel, Roustam Ibraguimbekov

Cast: Sandrine Bonnaire (Marie Golovine), Oleg Menchikov (Alexeï Golovine), Sergueï Bodrov Jr (Sacha), Catherine Deneuve (Gabrielle Develay), René Féret (the French Ambassador)

Director of photography: Laurent Dailland

Costume designer: Pierre-Yves Gayraud

Music: Patrick Doyle

Release date: 1999

Miss my flight. Wake up at quarter to nine, it's already light, was supposed to be up at seven to leave for Sofia. My alarm clock was still on New York time. Go back to sleep until 1 p.m., too tired to feel guilty. Have to take Austrian Airlines and change flights. Just to be safe, the assistant director comes with me as far as Vienna.

The air hostesses wear red from head to foot – even their tights. Little Red Riding Hoods. Official welcome to Sofia. Met by the studio head, fur-lined jacket, bouquet of flowers, photos, then outside are TV crews and fans holding photographs. Sunny, and not too cold. Set off for Plovdiv. Almost a hundred miles to the shoot. The Royal Hotel. Nicknamed the Royal Mafia. A small, brand-new hotel, pseudo chic – Eastern European luxury, nouveau riche, like they have in the East these days, like in Moscow.

Monday morning
Crisp blue sky. Bright-red coat and velvet beret; arrival by car at the hotel where I'll tell Sandrine/Marie's husband, Alexeï, that she can leave for France if she wants to. Almost the end of the film. Immediately feel like I'm back in *The Last Metro*. The German military command. Beautiful old hotel where part of the crew are staying. Big, red sofas, huge bar on the mezzanine floor, dark wood. Grand but also warm, and historically intact. Régis seems on good form. I watch the first screening on a TV set, already edited and set to music. Very promising. Laurent Dailland's photography is exquisite. Sandrine is magnificent, and stunning too, which is important in this

film. Régis has organised drinks on his landing. Very nice. He's a little stiff, which isn't unusual, he's always in control … but then I don't think that's a bad thing in these countries, which can pose a lot of difficulties, after all. Nice to walk into a film where I already know part of the crew. Lunch in the big hotel dining room, massive long tables set up in rows, the design all rather Stalinist. I joke around a fair bit, always trying to help Régis relax, because despite everything the atmosphere on set is still a bit tense. He does like discipline. You don't get over a military background just like that! My round-toed Minnie Mouse shoes, stockings, eyeliner and red lipstick all help me to become Gabrielle. Still haven't filmed much, and hardly any dialogue.

Yesterday, we filmed in the studio. A huge neo-classical building built in the 1960s apparently – I thought it was older. Dilapidated, but repainted for the shoot, cursorily done yet quaint. A great crowd of people, huge Bulgarian team, an interpreter for each crew – about a hundred of us. The ancient, wooden set is terribly noisy – reminds me of the old Boulogne-Billancourt studio. Filming car scenes against a blue background. Tedious work, and the technique also means the cutting will have to be done very precisely. Hurray for the theatre and embassy scenes. Sandrine and I compare notes: the heavy cutting, abstraction and lack of context do make it difficult work. Especially for her, surrounded by neon lights and in silence, with the camera so close, never mind the windshield. This is her big departure, her flight, her desertion, and she has to do it all in a bubble of light.

Huge presidential suite at the Kempinski Hotel, a few miles out of town, unfortunately. I'm not shooting today so I go into the city with the delightful Yavor, my driver and interpreter. It's snowing and less cold than it was.

Visit the St Nicolas Russian church. I light two candles and put them in front of these beautiful icons, for A. and C., may they be well, may I hold them even more strongly in my mind. Lunch at Krim, formerly a Russian club. Everything seems to feature peppers, cucumbers and pork! And it's all fatty. I fall back on tomato and feta salads and the hotel's Japanese restaurant.

Despite police surveillance, the generator got stolen last night in Plovdiv. Very serious. The Minister of Home Affairs got involved, it made the front pages, and then the generator was found, abandoned, ten miles out of town. Not only that, but the set was damaged yesterday by the driver of the thirty-tonne truck deciding to drive right into the studio, rather than unload the car that we were using for the shoot! Only a few hours' delay.

Today, we shoot on the border of the former Yugo-slavia, for the very end of the film. There's been a lot of snow; the journey takes an hour and a half. Hope it will be manageable. Luckily, there's no wind, the sun is strong behind the low cloud cover, the light is wonderful and the landscape so classic! The bridge, the uniformed guards, the German Shepherds looking quite different with their coats all white from the snow. For us, just a few shots in the old Mercedes. Waiting, papers, offi-cialdom. It's so cold when you're not moving, very glad I've got the heated insoles. Final shot. The car is all trussed up like a sled, so it can be pulled along by grips roped all the way along the bridge to avoid having to use a car-dolly; we wouldn't have had time, with the light falling so quickly. At 5 p.m. it's all over. The sign for 'Yugoslavia – 5 km' makes a real impression on me. All that horror happening so close by.

Sunday 22 November

Remarkable visit to the church at Boyana. I asked to go, we're shown round by the curator – it's a museum. Eighteenth-century frescoes, some being restored right now. Marvellous. Because it isn't open, the colours have stayed intact; they only need restoring because of the damage caused by the underground stream. In some places older frescoes peek through the more recent eighteenth-century depictions – a bizarre, intensely alive eye, a poignant Christ, St Nicolas, of course. Some of the faces have eyes that follow you around. Afterwards, in this arctic cold, we visit the Alexander Nevski cathedral. An Orthodox wedding is taking place. The bride is like a jovial Barbie doll, all in white, which is hardly 'orthodox'. They give us biscuits as we leave, seems more like a hasty benediction.

Monday 23 November

Although it was cold when we arrived, it was so sunny, then the snow, and now this leaden grey sky which, depressingly, matches everything – the houses, the potholed streets, the people. Sadness, even more than poverty. Night shoot at the theatre. My arrival at the police station in my marquis's costume. It has snowed, the scenery is so photogenic. Régis didn't film in the early evening. He wasn't happy with the set; the Russian set designer clearly hasn't managed to get the sets ready early enough. We change set almost every other day, whereas in Russia he sometimes has two years. Theatre dressing rooms – so realistic they make me a bit nervous – and these dressing tables surrounded by speakers, they're on, so we know they're working. Stage fright, even though we're only shooting backstage. Perhaps it also reminds

me of my childhood? This austere town, the 1950s ...
melancholy, and denial too.

Tuesday 24 November
Mary Tudor, auburn hair, stage make-up, gorgeous black
and gold costume, perfect for the theatre of the time. The
corset makes it horribly heavy. Today will be a long day,
and our work schedule is very tight.

Thursday 26 November
The palace of Tsar Simeon, outside Sofia. A huge, main-
tained residence, but in such a state! Freezing cold, in
the way that only unheated, uninhabited houses can be.
Marble staircase, which makes me feel even colder. We
use gas heaters that give me migraines. In my room I
roast tangerine skins in front of the heater, and burn rose
incense, which after a couple of days, makes it a bit
more appealing. But then it's time to leave. Post-war
atmosphere – that Polaroid of me on the sofa in front
of the heater, with a fur coat round my shoulders. My
character is a bit like a continuation of Marion in *The
Last Metro*, without the relationship complexity. This
film isn't about me. Gabrielle features at the beginning
and the end, living, making use of her immense power
and influence. More mature than me, that's for sure. I'm
still having trouble learning my lines impeccably. It's not
only laziness; it's also, I think, a desire to keep the shoot
fresh. Maybe I'm wrong. Being 'free' of script concerns
is definitely an asset, but I'm always nervous of the words
becoming mechanical, too quick, except in the case of
very long dialogues. Anyway, I need uncertainty in everything. But sometimes I create my own downfall, when
lack of familiarity with the script stops me focusing on
anything else. Filming always happens so quickly! And

at the moment I can feel Régis's hurry – four or five takes max. We need to make good progress, though he does make sure to capture the essentials of each shot, sometimes using two cameras – it saves time, and it feels so much more natural actually being with the other actor. Film the argument with the ambassador (René Féret), who is excellent, his slightly old-fashioned hairstyle and build are so well suited to the era. I'm always worrying that, because Régis tends to shoot from the front rather than from all around, the film could look a little rigid, rather like Régis himself. Laurent Dailland is shooting, I love the way he looks at things, so gentle and yet full of energy. If only they weren't so strict about silence on set, the atmosphere would be so much warmer. But in any case, it's all going well, though perhaps I'm tired, because the days seem to be dragging. Drinking a lot of tea, eating Petit Lu biscuits and chocolate – the canteen food isn't great. Struggling to fall asleep in the evenings.

Closing scenes, at the embassy. So few daylight hours. The wind is freezing, my whole face shrinks from it, and despite my foot-warming gel pads, all I'm thinking about (I am wearing seamed nylon stockings) is the end of each shot so I can get back into the warm. We don't stop for lunch, but we're right next to the Italian Embassy; they invite me over for pasta during the first break, and they serve it with a glass of white wine too – back outside I'm much better able to handle the cold for the final shots! Night falls so quickly, at four o'clock, light rain like melted snow. Even with two cameras we don't manage to finish the scene. We'll have to come back on Saturday, as that's the only day you're allowed to shoot in the road housing all the embassies, near the Alexander Nevski cathedral. Régis has great strength in adversity, as if he were alone against the world. Against everyone. I'm not totally present, but it doesn't really matter for today's shoot. Raise a concern about Sandrine's shoes – they look too 'clean'. It causes a whole fracas; Régis has another (I didn't know this was going on) argument with the costume and make-up department. But we are in Russia in the 1950s. Strangely, it seems that he gave way in the end. I know he wants Sandrine to be beautiful, but you have to give credence to the era and their lives in those communal apartments. Reconstructions are always a challenge – you have to invent some things and destroy others. For this same reason Régis wants to re-shoot one of Sandrine's scenes in the disused swimming pool. This issue sometimes came up with *Indochine*. I vow to pay more attention. To always prioritise the film. You can never think about it enough. Amazing performance from the Russian actor Oleg, he's learning his lines phonetically yet manages to really act. His coach writes out the lines for him in phonetic Cyrillic characters. Mind-blowing, and so brave. A very secretive actor, nervy and inscrutable, attractive. Masculine, yet also feminine?

Pinched an enamelled 1950s waste-paper bin from the theatre – it'll be glorious once it's repainted!

Snowing, this Saturday evening. Silence, softness, hidden poverty. In Sofia the snow is seductive. Sandrine threw a lovely party at the Blue House this evening. Tried to dance but I found it hard to join in, stayed on the edges; despite the delightful Hubert Saint-Macary, and me knowing part of the crew, I still feel as if I'm just passing through. It's not really my film. I'm only filming for three weeks. Don't quite realise this until I eventually get to shoot with Sandrine, the heroine. Not so easy. Better when I don't have to confront the situation directly. I'm not used to not being central, even for a short time. Although I have done several cameos this year: Carax, Carrel and soon Ruiz. I need to work less – and more.

Monday 7 December
No filming for me. Hang around. Sauna, shopping, get my hair coloured by Agathe. Learn to finish things. Study the script for Mary Tudor and this week's other scenes, because it'll all happen very quickly now.

Tuesday 8 December
Later start, which suits me. Rather worried about being on stage for a very theatrical scene in such a huge theatre. Today is the parliament scene, yesterday was the Communist Party headquarters. Four hundred extras. Minimalist set, black background, gilt banners, black sofa, black and gold costumes. Lighting very strong, dazzling the front row of the audience; it was designed so the camera could film from the stalls. Once again I'm reminded of *The Last Metro*.

Only a few takes, two cameras, no close-ups. Régis, who rehearsed me a little, didn't seem over the moon either.

Pleased tonight is behind us. I don't find it easy being on stage. Especially with the whole theatre being so well lit, almost to film levels.

The heavy costume binds me, affects my bearing. The corset makes me light-headed; the body is bound, and the brain as well. So many things you can't do wearing a corset, so much freedom shackled! It's a prison for the body, but also for the mind. The abolition of the corset was revolutionary!

Shoot at the theatre, as the marquis. Curtain call. Wooden floorboards, ancient stage that reminds me of the studio in Boyana. More realistic than any period stage we could have constructed.

Here we go again, Saturday 8.30 a.m., finishing the scene in front of the embassy. Beautiful blue sky. Have to break for lunch because the square is too sunny! Shoot at the university, set up as the French National Theatre's backstage area. Wearing a lovely black suit with flower-embroidered pockets, hair in loose curls to my shoulders. Only two shots, but it's already late. I feel present, but like I'm passing through. Before we film my last shot, Régis announces that I'll be leaving. Luckily, I don't have to say goodbye because the make-up and wardrobe crew are throwing a party tonight.

I must try and talk to Régis about the Serguei situation before I leave. Ideally, some of his dialogue should be dubbed. He speaks, but his French isn't fluent enough.

Night Wind

1998

Director: Philippe Garrel

Screenplay: Philippe Garrel, Xavier Beauvois, Marc Cholodenko, Arlette Langmann

Cast: Catherine Deneuve (Hélène), Xavier Beauvois (Paul), Daniel Duval (Serge), Jacques Lassalle (Hélène's husband)

Director of photography: Caroline Champetier

Costume designer: Elisabeth Tavernier

Music: John Cale

Release date: 1999

First day of filming, 27 April. Cold, windy, my hair's still wet when I arrive to do the set up, which Garrel has requested (at last!), before he positions the camera. Chronological shoot, rue du Mail, on the – very beautiful, simple – eighteenth-century staircase, facing the garden. I can tell he's happy and quite excited. Long salt-and-pepper hair, intelligent blue eyes full of laughter. Good-looking, former heart-throb, clearly lived it up. Theoretically, we're to rehearse so that if possible we only shoot once. He seems so sure of what he's doing, while still leaving a lot of space for spontaneity. We're filming in panoramic. 'Don't think about acting. Just dwell in the character's thoughts. Keep it simple; the thoughts are enough. If you think right, you'll be right.' Short day. It all feels free and simple. He doesn't want to constrain the actors in any way. The crew is light but comprehensive. All we're lacking is a script! He says he doesn't need one. 'Remember what you did in the last shot.' He never goes back over a scene. Wide shots, pan and two-person shots. A strange experience. You have to really be present; it's all over so fast.

Filming at the Villa Brune. Inside the tiny studio. With Xavier, as usual very pale, sharp, present, with whisky in his plastic cup. We have to kiss. 'If Catherine wants to!' says Philippe. Not really joking. A mattress on the ground, crumpled sheets. One take. Shot of Xavier in the bathroom. Me looking at the camera. Shot of Xavier watching me. Lots of short, strong shots – he doesn't want anything to become stale. Always the characters' thoughts. Not words. We explore together on this crowded set – the technicians are closer to me than Xavier is. It's a little oppressive, but there's also a great lightness. We're all very much making Garrel's film. He would have been quite happy to film at my place, or right nearby, using my own clothes. Not to be realistic but for simplicity's sake, because for him none of that counts for much. No colours. Nothing shiny. Elisabeth, the costume designer, and I are sometimes disconcerted by his flat rejections, right down to the stitching (too shiny). Xavier in the worn leather jacket Doillon gave him when they made *Ponette*. His wardrobe includes a lovely blue-grey shirt as well, though Philippe would happily have done without it. As far as I know there are also two jackets, a raincoat, a pair of perfectly polished shoes, and sparkling-white, unironed shirts. He's elegant, very attentive, intense.

Outdoor scene on the rue du Mail. No police presence. It's complicated, but he seems very happy, stopping the traffic with the help of his assistant, Aude, and the assistant director. The shots don't take long, but long enough for people to start blaring their horns. I ask him if its doing well, he seemed very excited (he hasn't filmed for three years): 'Yes, oh yes, I'm really on a roll now.' I'm happy, and a little disarmed at being onboard like this. I wanted this encounter; we had a project in the pipeline two years ago. Everything is bare and static; and on screen I find a certain intensity in these static shots. And he's taken on a cameraman so that Caroline Champetier can focus entirely on the light. After doing some tests, she chooses the Fuji, which gives the softest light. A few harsh shots (bad profiles, low camera). I'll suggest we do them again; I know he'll agree. Film a shot in the kitchen, I'm writing, eyes down, of course. A scarlet Formica table that he had tailor-made, like the Porsche

Daniel Duval drives, specially re-sprayed, like my coat, dyed to order.

Nerve-racking to have to frame and focus shots in a single take; only R. Levert on sound stays calm and relaxed. He listens closely and cedes easily when there are technical problems. He's so clear on the essentials. He marks his own positions with chalk, like a chief grip. It seems to me that he enjoys this working-man aspect of filmmaking. Practical craftsmanship. For luxury, we have panoramic, technicolour, and my huge trailer!

Indochine

1991

Director: Régis Wargnier

Screenplay: Régis Wargnier, Catherine Cohen, Lous Gardel, Erik Orsenna

Cast: Catherine Deneuve (Eliane Devries), Vincent Perez (Jean-Baptiste Le Guem), Linh Dan Phan (Camille), Jean Yanne (Guy Asselin), Dominique Blanc (Yvette), Henri Marteau (Emile Devries), Carlo Brandt (Castellani), Hubert Saint-Macary (Raymond), Andrzej Seweryn (Hebrard)

Director of photography: François Catonné

Costume designers: Gabriella Pescucci, Pierre-Yves Gayraud

Music: Patrick Doyle

Release date: 1992

Saturday 20 April

Arrive in Hanoi after twenty hours' travelling. Slept more than usual, it's colder than I was expecting. Leaden and luminous sky. Met on the tarmac next to the plane by a gorgeous car upholstered in crimson velvet. My driver speaks fluent French. Have to wait while the luggage goes through customs in a room full of stiff seats covered in white fabric, long tables and artificial flowers. Reminds me of the state VIP suites in Shanghai. Customs takes ages; I curl up for a little nap on one of the stiff benches.

Arrival at the hotel, seems like a carbon copy of a Cuban hotel! Built from grey stone, small fountains trickling on to bamboo plants, big flat pebbles, footbridges, a spiral staircase to a section of the first floor, ill-assorted and not that tidy, but the staff smile readily and seem to understand French quite well. The International Hotel, Hanoi. In any case, my suite is outside, a series of boxes on stilts linked to the main building by wooden footbridges over a large, muddy pond. Women and children with their trousers rolled up are busy plunging their arms in, searching for crabs, mussels and other creatures, some are fishing and the women on the banks work their nets till late at night ... women and children are clearly in the majority – also noticeable on the roads, where a lot of the repairs are done by women, wearing identical large hats and scarves to protect themselves from the dust. You can only tell their sex from the grace of their movements and bearing.

Late-afternoon visit to a place I call 'Cinecittà', where the whole production of the film shoot takes place, as well as the set-building and costume design. It's dilapidated, but large and spacious, and very atmospheric. The costume studio is incredible – a whole village (men and women) has been transplanted here to do the embroidery work for the ceremonial scenes. Very young men and women, whose silk-piercing gestures are brusque and, at the same time, finely measured; the unique sound of needles being pulled through fabric stretched out on bamboo that vibrates like a stringed instrument, under blue neon light. The cloth-dyeing studio, a large tiled room where the washerwomen are still dawdling, the cotton coloured with beautiful, natural dyes; and finally, the studios where masks, paper toys, birds and even hand-crafted furniture are being made, some to be sent on to Malaysia.

Dinner at 202 (a restaurant named after its street number), full of French people as the *Dien Bien Phu* film crew is here. Stuffed crab and bitter tea (make sure to ask for 'cooked' water), and back to the hotel through streets that are still teeming with life at 11 p.m.

I'm staying in Haiphong, in a wonderful place for only a dozen people, more of a house than a hotel, large airy rooms with ceiling fans and shuttered windows opening on to a balcony that runs the length of the building. Simple, but also luxurious – fridge, mosquito net and a large rug. I'm glad I brought my hundred-watt bulbs for evening reading.

Monday 22 April

Took the boat to where they're filming the fort scene: a wide, deep bay sheltered by sugar-loaf mountains, with dark-sailed sampans sometimes emerging like butterflies against the green water.

Magnificent set stolen from the coral boulders they

dynamited in order to create steps up to the summit, from where one can film along the two lines on which the set has been built, workmen's bamboo huts and landing stage on one side, office and hospital on the other. Wonderful in its simplicity, and as always, the small-scale crafts-manship evokes both fragility and strength, just like the people! The French canteen has been installed between the boats, like a barge, under a striped canopy, and we've got trailers made from buses mounted on boats, complete with fridges, beds and toilets. This all shows such minute attention to detail – they know the shoot will be long and are trying to make it as comfortable as possible. But I didn't anticipate it being as nice as this! They even sug-gested we bring our own soap, but my main preparations were culinary; just like the English, I brought yoghurts, honey and tea.

Tuesday 23 April
Last day of holidays before the first, well *my* first day of shooting, in Poulo Condor jail, some of the film's final scenes, or at least my last scene with Linh Dan – Camille, my daughter in the film. Hard to imagine anything more difficult – apart from the challenges of working in natural settings that can't be altered – than having to start with our farewell scene! Mustn't be afraid, got to trust in the scene, in its power.

Wednesday 24 April
Get up at 6.30 for this first day because the roads are bad and we have to take the ferry. Twenty or so miles takes almost an hour. Incredible scenery, the tide right out, vast expanses of mud presided over by a long pier where the prisoners and my Camille work and in the background those sugar-loaf mountains plunging into the sea like dark

coal walls. The black dust covers you before you can protect yourself, it's a larger-than-life extra in this film. Delays, mostly because the convict extras are too young to play political prisoners, and Régis refuses to shoot this crucial scene without the winding column of convicts, who represent a whole generation finally attaining freedom. Next come problems with the light – it's sunny, then cloudy. Simple set-up, because the scene will draw heavily on emotion, a long shot using a Steadicam followed by two close-ups, shot simultaneously on two cameras: we mustn't let this scene get stale.

I return to my bus and calmly go to sleep until they let me leave the set, as there's no longer any hope of shooting even the first shot. 5 p.m. Not a wasted day for everyone – the first part of the scene, without me, seems to have gone very well despite difficult conditions: the Vietnamese production department is very adept at manipulating and hiking up prices, and disregarding the needs of villagers. At 2 p.m. they hadn't eaten since early morning and were pulling their tunics over their heads as protection from the sun. It seems that the money meant for their lunch was not all spent as it should have been – sizeable misappropriations apparently – but relationships are sensitive and not to be treated lightly, as we'll be shooting here until 15 May.

Thursday 25 April
After a bad night's sleep, feel rather tired at the start of my first real day. Luckily, the morning shots cause delays, and I get an extra hour and a half in my bus. Régis briefs Linh Dan and me separately. The scene is a heavily emotional one, not much rehearsal, except for the extras – prisoners, soldiers, police (played by Russians and Bulgarians!); a long-lens camera and the Steadicam for

us two. From when I start running towards her, until her refusal to come with me. Régis wants to finish with an extreme close-up, using two cameras so as not to lose anything, and I'm grateful to him for not making us conserve our energy, for not having to remind him how important it is for actors to work quickly in emotional scenes. Leaden sky, no wind, and Régis briefing each of us right up to the last minute. I could feel his impatience with the cameraman working the Steadicam, the 'instrument' least under his control. Linh Dan's beauty has been so devastated by her ordeal that I have trouble recognising her in the stream of prisoners (I'm pleased to have suggested the white streak, like an emotional wound in her dark hair). After very few takes, the light abandons us, we're unable to finish the scene. I know it's hard, especially for her (I'm just listening), but we've got no choice, so we'll have to make the best of it.

Friday 26 April
The fates are with us, with me – I slept a lot, maybe eight hours straight, which hasn't happened for a long time. The light didn't match yesterday's until the afternoon, so I had plenty of time to prepare. In the end, the weather is often a blessing – we didn't have to finish the scene in a hurry as we would have done last night, which is a good thing, given the anguished and crucially important dialogue. Régis was more demanding today and, despite the emotional intensity, made us go over it more than he would probably have done yesterday; also the scene became longer, which seems to me more fitting to the agony of that last separation.

I know that I'm liked and admired; I can sense it, but in a warm way – everyone seems to feel they're working on an important film, not that that guarantees anything, but what a pleasure to immerse oneself in real scenes, properly directed and produced. The costumes for the crowd scenes are stunning, exquisitely hand-dyed. Pierre-Yves's task has been Herculean, he's been starting at dawn every morning, but he knows the effort will show. Felt light and relaxed as I boarded the ferry tonight to return to the hotel. It was almost dusk, 7.30, and I'm already used to whizzing along the road amid trucks, cars, bicycles, buffaloes pulling carts and all these people – always so industrious, never empty handed, they never leave anything behind, everything is taken, transformed and recycled.

Saturday 27 April
Dinner dance at the hotel, until dawn. Olivier, the assistant producer, in charge, the theme was 'Lou Reed and Tom Waits' – a bit stilted, but we did carry on till 3 a.m. Any calories from the champagne must have been spent during the first dance – I was soaked!

Linh Dan radiant, childlike, intelligent, with her crazy laugh and those adorable dimples. Vincent handsome, pure, mysterious. Such a subtle man.

Andrzej Seweryn, with a new crew-cut, unrecognisable, like a traditional, pure-bred Pole, dancing like an acrobat, shirt drenched in an instant, and that irresistible accent.

A wonderful production team, friendly and passionate about their work. They happily do eighteen-hour days, under the calm but rigorous guidance of Régis, whose sole commitment is to the film and its actors. A generous bloodsucker – thoughtful, but still the son of an army officer!

We're about to leave Ha Long Bay and our peaceful, airy family hotel. High in the mountains is a large square building, which I am told is a sanatorium. Coal mining is still practised on a large scale here, and it takes its toll. Long and arduous journey – bicycles constantly in the way, and it takes us five hours to travel 100 miles! Three ferry journeys, at times jam-packed with carts, children, chickens, trucks. Torrential rain in Hanoi, it's almost thirty degrees.

Tuesday 30 April

To 'Cinecittà'. Embroidery studios still fascinating, carpenters finishing off the catafalques. The red lacquer pillars are carved from the block, just as carefully as the costumes are hand-embroidered. I wonder how Régis will manage to include all these beautiful details when the schedule at Hué is so tight (one day for the riverside funeral, one day for the assassination of the Mandarin!) and the scenes already so complex – I wish he had four cameras.

Arrival at the village. Hordes of women, children, old people and zebus;[1] the children, though shy, follow us around; the women are beautiful and smile easily. Roads all paved in brick, houses mostly built from stone, with ornate entrances. Water everywhere, ducks, the stunning green of aquatic plant life, and then we come to the main house. Simple tea ceremony before visiting the embroiderers, who on this particular day are working in the pagoda, which looks like a huge inner courtyard. A magical sight. They take hardly any notice of us, concentrating on their detailed work, embroidering tunics for the marriage ceremony – dragons, mountains, clouds. The pieces of cloth are stretched tight, and the men and women work together on a whole panel, sitting

1 Type of Vietnamese cow.

43

cross-legged opposite each other. It's 6 p.m. There's no electricity, they tell me that the night shift will soon take over.

We run into a few difficulties as we try to leave, because the local police haven't been warned of our visit and we were supposed to tell them – ask for permission, in fact – before leaving Hanoi district. The official insists on taking a statement, even though he's the embroidery manager's brother. Plenty of slow tea-drinking. Pierre-Yves Gayraud (in charge of the Vietnamese costumes) lets us go on ahead, staying to deal with the formalities so we don't have to wait another half-hour. Blood-red sky and another intense storm. Takes more than an hour to get back to Hanoi, passing cycle rickshaws that are sheathed in plastic but still pedalling. They never stop.

Friday 3 May
Back to Cinecittà studio to try on the Indo-Chinese outfit I would like to wear in the pagoda scene when I go to make offerings after Camille disappears. It seems to me that there aren't many opportunities to show how 'native' Eliane is, and a place of worship seems appropriate. The wardrobe assistant Alberto jokes that he's worried about the Joan Crawford effect. It's true that on Europeans these outfits can easily look like fancy dress. In any case, what Gabriella has suggested – a severe but very beautiful navy-blue outfit – is almost tunic-like and so doesn't stand out among all the costumed extras. The heat is humid and very oppressive. I try on a superb chestnut-brown embroidered tunic, made for someone else but it could easily be altered to fit me perfectly. Black trousers, silk turban. I suggest to Régis that we try them both out on set, among the other women.

Saturday 4 May
Lunch with Vincent at old Hanoi restaurant Chaka. One dish, a kind of miso soup with fish (Chahe). He's very handsome, gorgeous, with a dazzling, tender smile clouded by eyes that are often solemn, and sometimes distracted. He seems serious and discreet. He started with the most difficult scenes – his long, drifting journey with Camille. 'States of being', rather than acted scenes as such.

Sunday 5 May
When we visit the few antique dealers, we really feel the effects of the *Dien Bien Phu* crew having been here for six months! In any case, it's illegal to export antiques, but I like to buy a few objects to decorate my bedroom with and so remember the film.

Dinner this evening at the French Embassy with Ambassador Blanchemaison. Nine French guests and a large Vietnamese delegation, but still a fairly relaxed evening. The Minister of Foreign Affairs was apologetic about having to leave before dinner; apparently they're hosting an important conference later this month. The officials in charge of cinema, television and radio were present, and I sat next to the Minister of Culture. Naturally, he told me of the difficulties they experience in meeting all their targets, and explained that they were only just starting to implement a legal structure to protect their works of art, which explains the occasional excesses of zeal: 'You live in a state governed by laws; whereas we come from a tradition of customs.' And it's true that these laws are strict, and, he adds, there's been thirty years of war ... they're a tight community, very shrewd, and clever, of course. And everywhere I go I get the impression that despite considerable difficulties they never give up – remaining subtle, supple, and with amazing stamina. Even in the cities it's not hard to imagine how the Americans lost the war.

Monday 6 May

Leave about 10 a.m. My throat hurts – too much air-conditioning, and the heat, but at least I don't speak in today's scene. We head for China Thay to film in a village or, more precisely, an old pagoda which I'll visit with offerings for Camille's safety. The villages here seem mediaeval – the one we're filming in is unbelievably calm and mysterious, hemmed in by huge, black, plant-covered rocks, with the pagoda in the middle of a lake, and children swimming in the murky water. Surrounded by mud-and-thatch houses, many with tiny stalls outside. Régis is waiting for me. It's already thirty-five degrees and no one has been allowed into the pagoda – he wants me to discover it first. What an extraordinary place! Two gloomy buildings, low-ceilinged, with enormous columns, bamboo awnings, and in the back, altars with giant statues whose faces transfix me with their expressiveness, like theatre masks. The statues are so huge they seem to have been set there before the walls themselves. Buddhist nuns on their mats, more lilies, incense. There'll be a long shot of me behind these statues, some towering like judges, and then coming to pay my respects at the altar, offering (Régis thought of this today) a jewel that I had wanted to give to Camille and that we will have seen at the beginning of the film, in happier times. It's easy to concentrate in such a setting. I'm dreading Malaysia, I know the scenery will be magnificent, but the atmosphere? Here, you can feel the spirituality of the people, and so far tourism hasn't taken over either Hanoi or Ha Long Bay. I'll see about Saigon on Thursday.

We'll have to shut all the doors tonight; the bullfrogs have started up their croaking. Someone must have told Régis he has green eyes – every day he wears green trousers and a turquoise t-shirt like a surgeon, but you can tease him about it, which is nice given his total commitment to the film. Everyone is doing their absolute utmost, but as soon as the actors arrive to rehearse, we become his top priority – you feel quicker, more immediate, you have his total attention.

He travelled four thousand miles by minibus to research the locations, only eighteen months ago. When I see the state of the roads, and this whole crew filming – already – I'm reminded that there are still enough madmen and people of goodwill to make this kind of cinema. Because it's an expensive film, though justifiable because it's so ambitious cinematographically, and the film will be three hours long, we can't afford any unforeseen problems – we can't go over schedule, no one is allowed to get sick, we're almost all irreplaceable. Anyway, I packed my trunk with bread, biscuits, honey and special long-life yoghurts from the French Institute for Agronomy Research. Even the rats like them – one evening in my room, I heard and then saw them carefully cutting through the metal lids – but I like rodents.

Tuesday 7 May
A quiet day, but oppressive and humid. In the early evening, we decide to return to the village to watch the others film the open-air theatre scene. A wonderful set made of cardboard and Chinese lanterns, with 200 extras sitting on benches near the pagoda in front of a small lake. A really magical scene, lit by oil lamps. The show, nerve-rackingly, had been selected from books by Régis and Catherine Cohen in Paris. Régis was lucky and

persistent enough to find a small Hanoi theatre troupe willing to tailor the production and the acting to his interpretation and subsequent description.

I start to worry a little on the way when I see lightning flashing closer and closer from the same direction as the village. I arrive just as they begin to film, after substantial rehearsing. A 1.3-metre dolly and a second camera for close-ups. The whole play will be filmed and then cut. Set design, make-up, costumes, musicians, an extravaganza of colour, character play, Princess Linh Dan unrecognisable under her make-up and crown, her handmaiden, three warriors and musicians everywhere. A blend of realism and fairy tale; he'll do two takes. A few drops of rain start to fall, parasols are put up. Vincent has been waiting in his caravan, stunningly made up as a warrior (two and a half hours' work). He takes shelter too, and suddenly the wind flares up, exploding the lamps. Like a cyclone. Torrential rain beats down on us, the set almost totally collapses, no one has time to take shelter, and those who put away the equipment look like drowned rats by the time they reach the tarpaulined canteen. Muddy almost immediately, three inches of rain, everywhere clogged up, cold-drink crates floating around, I see a kitchen worker draining pasta in the rain! In steam that seems to be coming out of nowhere.

The water starts to penetrate your skin, almost all the men are bare-chested, the women have a worse time of it because they don't take their tops off at night and so nothing will dry. Régis stays calm, smiling, surreal – no sign of panic or upset. Probably due to the scale of the disaster, which seems almost like divine punishment, but also largely thanks to the excellent atmosphere on the shoot. You can really tell the nature of a shoot at difficult moments. Rabbit pasta, brie, a slightly runny but delicious chocolate mousse. No one cold-shoulders these pleasures or the crowdedness of the space; this 'state', shared by everybody, creates an extraordinary togetherness. Alberto, half-naked, is wearing the crown on his head – to protect it? Feels more like a party than a disaster.

No chance of starting again; the rain goes on for over an hour. There's talk of lodging with local people, as the final five miles of road is in very bad shape. More waiting. But then our car leaves after all, first, scouting out the way, with Han sometimes turning up his trousers and checking the road barefoot before driving on it. Hanoi is the worst, some areas totally flooded, and we have to turn around a dozen times to avoid particular streets. The final street is half-blocked by an uprooted tree which looks just like an old sleeping giant. The last 'straight' stretch is the most risky, it's the only remaining option for getting to the hotel so we have to take it, and even going very slowly the car could get stuck – I know the water is up to mid-calf. We inch through, and I have to leap on to the bungalow path. The sight of Han, barefoot with his trousers rolled up to his knees, politely wishing me goodnight. It's taken us almost two hours. The bullfrogs are going wild, and intense lightning is flashing across the sky above the city. It's Hanoi, but it feels like Baghdad. It's raining on my bed; the roof couldn't hold it off completely. But I still sleep, a little, though this morning's sore throat hasn't cleared up at all. I'll have to start antibiotics. Luckily, I'm not filming. The bicycle really is king here – tonight only they and the cycle rickshaws could easily negotiate a flooded Hanoi, filling the air with the strange whistle of wet tyres, multiplied so many times it sounded like a swarm of insects.

Friday 10 May

Night-time, everyone is on the stage. But it's a delicate scene. I decide to leave once I've blown a kiss to my daughter. I can only make out her face, and Vincent's, their theatrical masks blending just before the birth that will unite them, fusing their real faces together in the heat and Camille's cries.

Monday 13 May

Leave Tang Loy around 8 a.m. for a charter flight to Danang, we'll drive the last two hours to Hué. Big mini-drama at the airport: probably due to lack of space, my hats and clothes were rolled up in a brown-paper package at the last minute; when Alberto, despairing, opened it on the airport floor, the cloth and straw were totally crushed. Control myself because I can feel Régis's rising fury. And the padlocks were broken to raid the trunk! I'm sickened: the chiffon funeral veil is all ripped, the broad-brimmed hat probably beyond repair, very frustrating. I still fall asleep an hour into the car journey, wiped out by the heat once we cross the cloud barrier where some of the crew will be filming.

A half-hour climb, twenty porters, challenging, the ground pitted with mines and infested with snakes, but near-perfect weather makes the long, hard effort worth it. Camille and the Sao family discovering the coast after their climb, and then the sea. The coastline is gorgeous, little deserted beaches, green hills.

Arrival at the Hotel Hu' O'ng Giang, lots of smiling young girls, hostesses, masseuses? Monique, my interpreter, must have already made contact because there's a new honeymoon bedspread in my room and a big Chinese chest of drawers inlaid with mother-of-pearl. Comfort: a rug, a fridge and a spa bathroom. White lotus flowers and huge picture windows opening on to the Perfume River – sampans, small craft, a lagoon – a gorgeous, romantic view, and the room is very spacious. I know I'll sleep well here; feels a bit like Bay Chay.

Dusk visit to the Imperial City. With the bureaucracy and delays of the system, it's taken the set-design crew four months to repaint and repair the balusters, fill up the ornamental lakes and mount the submerged water lilies on bamboo stems fastened to the bottom, so they can move around on their willow cradles with remarkable agility. The lakes are almost finished, it's magnificent, the red and yellow frescoes in the main pavilion seem as though they've always looked this fresh. I'm quite emotional, anticipating tomorrow's shoot when I arrive in the city never yet penetrated by a European, the flags, the guards, the walk through the state reception rooms. This is perhaps the first time a European film has ever been shot in the Imperial City of Hué, former capital of the country. Régis arrives in the evening, exhausted but happy, the sun came out to shine almost exactly when he wanted it. He tells me about the shoot, the strong feelings of the family as they reach the summit and freedom.

Wednesday 15 May
Up at 6.30 a.m. Important scene, the funeral on the river. With all these boats and funeral processions I'm sure it's going to be a very long shoot despite yesterday's rehearsals. First in line are the two standard-bearing boats. Next come the 'sentances' burning incense, the red-lacquer catafalque, me all in black and little five-year-old Camille, in her white embroidered dress, then the offerings boat, then boats bearing the musicians dressed in white and purple. Not a breath of wind, even on the water. I daren't ask the temperature. We spend more than

two hours on the first shot: the choreography of the rowing boats and the incense-smoke effects make the eight-minute shot extremely complicated. We only do two whole takes. Throughout the morning I can feel my little Camille swaying from heat and exhaustion, I try to fan her as much as possible. I watch her eyes closing even when she's standing up, but she's impeccably con-scientious. I don't think I've ever been this hot in my life.

Like monasteries, pagodas are built in very precise locations chosen for the landscape and the light. 5.30 p.m., end of the shoot. I notice Régis bend over, grey, hugging himself. 'I knew I had just filmed a burial.' He was so pale that I thought he was sick. He'd just been told of the death of his terminally ill brother. He'd said to me before leaving for Vietnam that he knew it was going to happen, but that he wouldn't be able to return home. Nothing to do except stay with him, listen to him, so much going on, happening all at once, so chaotic. Vincent, François, Claudine, Linh Dan and I have a talk, we suggest changing the schedule because he can't shoot the assassination of the Mandarin. It's already 8 p.m., and everything's so complicated here. If we cancel the extras, we'll only get their reply at 11 a.m. tomorrow at the earliest. He has to phone, I offer to take him to Hué post office. Notice for the first time that he's left-handed, though he's trembling so much that I have to write down the numbers. Ten interminable minutes with a charming operator in the huge, Soviet-like post office. He looks at me, remarks that I've taken on the lavender hue of the walls. It's true, we smile, and then to cabin number 3 for six minutes. I pull the dollars out of his pocket so that I can pay while he flees to the dark of the car as quickly as possible.

Thursday 16 May

Hard to wake up. 6.45 a.m. Sleepy. We've moved on to a calmer scene at last, at the lotus lake. My stilted reconciliation with Camille, in retreat to prepare for her marriage – a dark, tidy-haired, completely inaccessible little princess. Linh Dan's voice is the only childlike thing about her in this slightly mannered passage. The surroundings are so tranquil, so beautiful – once again, they've planted white and pink lotus flowers during the night. We're sitting looking out from a little pavilion facing the pagoda. These places feel so lived-in that it's impossible not to immerse oneself in the scenes. How will I manage in the studio? Well, Régis will be there, telling me a story before each important shot, I know he'll be like that to the end, today more than ever. Yesterday, he told me not to worry about the film! He knows very well that I'm not worried, it's him we have to take care of. Today and every day.

Friday 17 May

Assassination of the Mandarin in the Courtyard of the Urns. The Imperial City.

Fiery red dress, black garden-party-style hat. My bus is like a furnace, so I come out to wait in the fresh air of the pagoda, next to the courtyard where we're filming. Not a breath of wind, my chiffon dress is already marked where it's sticking to my skin. The huge bronze urns filled with incense, a long tracking shot right to the steps of the pavilion where the Mandarin (a doctor!), his young wife, and the black-robed nobility are sitting. Tense atmosphere, Régis is very nervous yet well behaved because, apart from Henri Marteau playing my father (he's like someone from the nineteenth century, *Death in Venice*?), none are professional actors, which will pose

problems for the rest of the day. Intimidated and com-
pulsively smiling, the women are unable to act terror-
stricken when the assassination takes place. I sense that
Régis, who has already postponed this shoot, is reluctant
to start on it. He does start, and he will do it. But the
confusion and total lack of sophistication of the extras
allow him to further simplify this scene that he hadn't
wanted to think about. Around 3 p.m. he takes a quiet
moment in one of the pagodas. I nearly crush the Mandarin when I throw myself at him just after he's been
shot – the seat tips, he falls, which wasn't supposed to
happen. I don't know how I manage to continue the
scene, we laugh like maniacs for a quarter of an hour
before being able to start again. I'm exhausted, mainly
from the heat, and we have to rush the last scene as the
first drops of rain start falling.

Monday 10 June
First day at the plantation. Grey sky, muggy, dense palm
groves, rubber trees, clearings, tapping the trees, the
rubber flowing slowly out, white and milky, into small
dishes, smelling like tofu or sour milk, the coolies wearing
head torches because they start work at daybreak, dawn
mist; it's magnificent. In less than half an hour my lovely
blue linen blouse is sticking to my skin, but even in a hat
and jodhpurs I find this humidity easier than the sun!
The riding-crop scene, the coolie on his knees – he's so
handsome! The tracking shot that pans on to us won't
show me hitting him, but I'll still seem like the proverbial
good paternalistic master who 'punishes out of love'. I
sense that Régis will do more takes of Vincent's scene, so
that he can edit our first real meeting extensively. The
days are hard work, and long as well – we spend more than
an hour in the car each day. And yesterday's torrential

downpour flooded the city, making access to the shoot difficult: we have to travel in jeeps. We're running a day late because the mist-making lorry can't get here, meaning that we'll miss the morning of our first day in Malaysia. The producer Eric Heumann is furious, and I can see why. Unfortunately, there's nothing we can do apart from support Régis in his decision not to shoot without the mist. The jungle atmosphere, the whole magic of the scene would be lost, especially the appearance of Jean-Baptiste, dressed in white like an archangel!

Tuesday 11 June
Arrival at the factory. What beauty, but what madness too, such a sumptuously realistic, perfectly made set for a week-long shoot, luxurious, a real office, a factory with functioning machines. All the accessories and costumes are beautiful, accurate, real, and that's the difference. Although the days are demanding (proper scenes only, not a single transition scene), Régis makes sure the crew encourages the actors and the actress, and shows consideration. Long tracking shot. The courtyard is overwhelmingly hot, it must be forty degrees by midday, or nearly. I've been hot before but I've never given off this much liquid!

Dominique Blanc has arrived to do her big exit scene. Long integral shot. She leaves like a Parisienne – print dress, pearl necklace, plant and birdcage! The scene itself is well written, but she really is fantastic. Régis truly loves the actors, and he's crazy about his film. I don't know when he takes a break. He's still in meetings at nine at night, tense ones sometimes, taking it all upon himself, almost too much. But I can sense his enjoyment and how seriously he takes his responsibilities. A unique film, in an extraordinary country, with a huge budget, and he's got to make it work. As simple as that! We're very close, we talk a lot, especially in the evenings. He gets me talking about myself, he's got a talent for it. Ten years of psychoanalysis! But his curiosity is real, and he's very attentive. He takes, demands in fact, but also gives me a great deal.

The factory is far away, nearly two hours' drive in dreadful traffic packed with crazy motorcyclists. The set is superb, as beautiful as a child's model of a factory, perfect. I can hardly believe these hyper-developed sets when we're only going to be shooting for a week at most! The black gravel courtyard is extremely hot, and there's a lot of reverb. We shoot through the hottest hours because I can't work too early in the morning – I got them to promise me that in France – and the light fades at six in the evening. Permanent fans are installed in the courtyard. I'm baking, even though I'm not wearing a wig and the dresses are chiffon, but there's also the heat from the rubber factory, and I am wearing a red dress. Settle into my office, with two fans and my feet on the table. Find Yvette's bird dead in its cage: it was left behind on Sunday without any water. I think of *Mississippi Mermaid*, I was already reminded of it when she left the office in her silk dress, carrying the cage. The heat slows the shoot. We're not managing to finish the scenes, even the fire scene. We had to stop before the end, after overrunning for an hour. I hope we'll reach a compromise of four takes max, unless there are technical difficulties.

The gunboat and burning sampan scene will have to be shot at night, we'll do it tomorrow, and then stop until Thursday. It's going to be hard work returning to all the unfinished scenes in a race against the clock. The work schedule is too heavy. Every scene is an important one, we need more time.

vingt,deux octobre mil neuf cent quarante-trois, treize heures trente-... est née, 22, Cité des Fleurs, Catherine Fabienne, du sexe féminin, Georges Maurice Edmond DORLÉAC, né à Paris 6e le vingt-six mars mil ... cent un, artiste dramatique, et de Renée Jeanne DENEUVE, née au ... ... (Seine-Inférieure) le dix septembre mil neuf cent onze, artiste dra-... son épouse, domiciliés 69, boulevard Exelmans. Dressé le vingt-... mil neuf cent quarante-trois, seize heures quarante-cinq, sur ... du père, qui, lecture faite a signé avec Nous, Jean Edouard ... SCHWENCK, adjoint au Maire ... septième arrondissement de Paris,

1674.   *Dorléac*

Marié à Londres le 18 août 1965 avec David Royston BAILEY. Acte transcrit le 16 septembre 1965 au Consulat Général de France, à Londres, le 9 Décembre 1965. Le Greffier

Divorcée de David Royston BAILEY par jugement rendu le 24 juin 1970 par le Tribunal de Grande Instance de Paris, — Transcrit le 20 novembre 1970 au Ministère des Affaires Étrangères à Nantes (Loire Atlantique) le 23 février 1974

Below: Françoise and me in my mother's arms, out of town on the banks of the Seine.

My little sister Sylvie and me.

With my sisters Françoise and Danielle, on the balcony of our apartment on boulevard Exelmans.

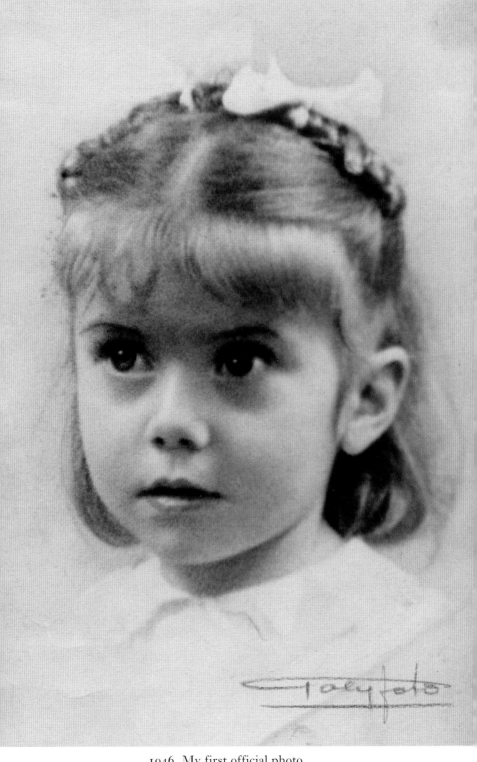

1946. My first official photo.

1946. Summer holidays.

With old friends in Saint-Hilaire.

More photos taken by my dad, so delighted with 'his girls'.

1947. Catherine, Danielle, Françoise. Those stiff little post-war coats.

1948. Françoise, my father, Sylvie, Danielle and me. Rompers and stripy jumpers. Summer camping at Blonville in Normandy.

1950. I'm seven.

One of my dad's favourite photos
– all the important women in his
life.

Lamazou School.

Mine and Françoise's first communion: like a little bride.

No more milk teeth. Smiling with our mouths shut.

1951.

School photo.

Below: Our life as a family.

First overseas trip, to Hastings in England. Supposedly to learn English.

The sixties.

Françoise and me at our elder sister's wedding.

Going to a screening with my parents; I've gone blonde.

Around the time of my first film, *The Door Slams*, in 1960.

Yesterday, the technical adviser was showing Henri Marteau how to hand-flatten raw rubber before putting it through the machines. Unpleasant smell of fermented tofu, but the smoking process makes it blond and golden like tortoiseshell. Eric Heumann called to reassure Régis about the delays. Will he manage to carry on being so courageous? I hope he'll be able to remain this bold and daring throughout; you have to be a bit crazy to be a producer. Hope I'll eventually get to see the rushes with this local crew, in about ten days' time. Even if there's no sound, I need concrete confirmation of the characters and the atmosphere. Need to see. Also to hear, I hope, though I keep asking Guillaume, the sound engineer, whether the last take was OK. This is perhaps the first time I've felt as involved with and, at the same time, responsible for a film written for me and with this level of budget; it's a big challenge, an incredible gift that gives me satisfaction every day without my having to do anything. A real daily pleasure, like with *The Last Metro*. I also feel very well physically, even at just under fifty-four kilos (eight and a half stone), which is a bit light for me. My figure looks good, right for the period, though it's a bit tough on the face, especially as the heat and lack of sleep don't do the eyes any favours. Everyone has been affected, but I hope it will only be noticeable on the documentary about the making of the film. The actor's paradox and self-imploding challenge in these conditions, so unusual and extreme: show everything but show nothing that could interfere with the scene or the character.

Wednesday 12 June
Night shoot. I go to join them for dinner. The gunboat in dock, Vincent and Thibaut handsome in their white uniforms, so youthful and authentic. Régis rather tense.

Lots of noise on the river – the ferry and the fishermen. It's a difficult scene, and the sound issues cause another half-hour's delay. There's the tide to consider, which is likely to create problems until 3 a.m. But they also have to burn the sampan, and they won't finish until seven in the morning. So a change in my schedule – I'll only be rehearsing my first scene with Mrs Minh Tan. The production department is worried: three days' delay during a ten-day period, but the schedule is extremely tight, and there are so many scenes. We can't do any better considering the size of the production – 230 people, I think – which is extremely cumbersome and hard to move around. And this isn't Vietnam; people aren't very dynamic. America yet not America. When we arrived at the village yesterday, I felt the real atmosphere of the film for the first time in Malaysia, that feeling we had in Hanoi and Ha Long Bay – so present and yet so far away. Vincent is magnificent, intense, in his difficult and literary scene; his theatre experience is a great support. And always those soft, solemn eyes.

Thursday 13 June
Cheong Fatt Tze.

Filming in Georgetown, our first time in a Malaysian city. An extraordinary Chinese mansion restored especially for the film. Ochre, red, turquoise pillars, everything has been repainted, the furniture and ornaments are perfect; all for just two days of shooting, what madness, what wonderful madness. The terrace, the grand staircase, the hundred-year-old bonsai trees in the middle, busy office to one side, living room and ancestral altar to the other.

Friday 14 June
We rehearsed the first scene yesterday, and it was rather difficult. Minh Tan isn't a professional actress, and Régis was very directive, perhaps too much so – she was out of her depth; I could feel her starting to tremble. Together, we decided to take another approach: stop her smiling, and let her just get on with saying her script, and we'll dub it later. It's a relief, because her scenes are important ones, and she isn't someone who'll improve on the actual shoot. We needed more time than we had. We were rehearsing at the Cathay Hotel, a dilapidated 1930s masterpiece, with a spa at the end of the hall and young women knitting to music under pink neon lights – waiting for clients? Of course, it all seemed more authentic on the set and especially with the costumes. But her face looked much harder once she was wearing the embroidered Indo-Chinese costume, with her hair pulled back into a severe bun, and her compulsive smiling. Régis had the clever idea of getting her to speak in Vietnamese, which helped mask the gaps in her acting. She was actually very good in the final scenes. But what an incredible risk for such an important role. My large blue-and-white straw hat offers fairly good protection for crossing the baking-hot courtyard on the way to the shoot. White chiffon dress with a blue pattern, bias cut and a lovely length with these very feminine, broad-brimmed hats; I only hope I won't look too elegant.

Saturday 15 June
Filming of the day after my opium session. In the hallway, no concealer under the eyes, greasy hair and dark glasses. I ask Régis to let me be more dazed than the script indicates – it had me standing up, restless, which I can't see as being compatible with opium, even forty-eight

hours later. Especially as you only see the end of the smoking session, and it's perhaps the only time we ever see Eliane truly broken. Even hurt and suffering, she's usually very proactive. Régis agrees; we struggle with Minh Tan, but the scenes are very hard, even for a professional. You have to move, speak and smoke at the same time, with total confidence and authority. I can sense she's very frightened, and he sometimes tries to rush her. We shoot more footage than anticipated so that we can use different takes, and by the end of the day she's even quite good, probably only a few sections will need dubbing, maybe by Minh Tan herself. The set is divine, with stencilled walls (that we'll have to abandon in two days' time!). I go up to the first floor, which hasn't been renovated, coffered ceilings, Liberty green-and-blue stained-glass windows, in very bad condition, but glorious. The lime-washed blue walls remind me of Seville and also North Africa, those purplish blues, faded ultramarine, Marrakech, Berber blue. Remains of tiles and Chinese enamel ornaments.

The streets are baking hot; wearing black silk pyjamas and a pink embroidered kimono, I find myself wandering back to the Cathay Hotel, people are strolling about in their shirt sleeves, yet it's me who feels at home. Reality is the world of the film, everything outside the film is outside me, Paris is far away, Europe even further, and apart from Antoine Blondin and Jerzy Kosinski dying, I'm not much bothered about what's happening in the world. I'm not visiting this film: I'm living in it, and sometimes next door, at the hotel, but never far away, and as one might expect, the film belongs to me; Régis offered it to me, I took it and we share it with great delight.

Thursday 20 June

Lengthy integral shot. Jean-Baptiste returning to ask me to look after the child, our first scene since the slap on Christmas Day. I ask to wear the Indo-Chinese tunic I bought at Hué, it used to belong to the family of Emperor Bao Dai. The light gets the better of us; we have to shoot Vincent's final close-up inside the room instead of with him looking back, framed in the sunlight, as he leaves – the last time I see him alive. What a shame. Régis isn't quite satisfied, but there were so many problems today. Ready for 12.30, integral shot of Vincent's return, our last scene together before his death. The technical department let us down: not enough power. They think they can get hold of some building-site generators for tomorrow, but in what condition? I can tell Régis is a bit frustrated – we had to wait so long to do this scene that by the time we've done four takes, he can sense we've nothing left to give, and it's true, but I think he would like to have done one more. He's frustrated, and so am I. What's more, I couldn't find him this evening to pass on all the positive feedback my agent Bertrand gave me on the most recent screening. Over here, we haven't seen anything since the Hué screening three weeks ago, and they don't understand that in Paris. It's good, they're telling us it's good, and therefore we should be reassured and satisfied. But they're not the ones 'doing' the film; they don't realise the impact of the lack of equipment, of not being able to alter, evaluate or improve things. But anything else is unthinkable – too much manpower and thus expenditure. What was bearable in Vietnam no longer is here.

Friday 21 June

11 p.m. Long-awaited screening in the hotel ball-room abandoned: the horrible quality of the lens made

everything blurred. We wasted an hour, and then gave up after the first reel. Régis and I decide to ask for a tape copy – with sound – for next week. I send Bertrand a fax and receive an affirmative reply the same evening. At last! While they check the reliability of the new generators, Linh Dan and I shoot her confession scene in the winter garden, a night scene, tarpaulined, lit by oil lamps. It's a short scene but very demanding, especially for Linh Dan as she has to break down and sob. Régis soon decides to use two cameras; François doesn't object to this additional challenge, graciously abandoning the effect of lamplight on our faces. It's really great when you can feel everyone respecting what's most needed for the good of the film. Only three takes, and it's true what I was saying to Vincent: even when you go all out for the other person's close-up, you're acting for their sake, to support them, rather than acting together.

Three tables set for twelve, the women beautifully made up, extremely elegant, a delightful Christmas scene. I have two shots – the first, and the last, at ten to midnight: long live cinema! Luckily, I sleep in between because we only get back to the hotel at two in the morning.

Saturday 22 June
The tango shoot. I reassure Linh Dan, telling her there'll be at least four shots, and two cameras, and reaction shots, and anyway, we're not at Bercy Stadium dancing live in front of 20,000 people – if we make a mistake, they'll just cut. She's more confident today. Just done the first shot where I lead her on to the dance floor for our tango demonstration, profile to profile, close-up, with the guests behind us watching. I tried not to let myself get overwhelmed!

The tango went well; we became more confident as the

takes progressed, despite the three cameras and the crowd of people! Once edited I'm sure it'll be perfect. Régis decides to do the altercation and the slap in a single shot; we'll go over time tonight. I feel almost chilly, my villa stands on a big hill, white clouds are streaming towards us, it's 11 p.m. and they breeze right into the house, like ghosts. I find a sofa and try to doze on set to conserve my strength. All the extras have gone, the only person with us is Linh Dan, who asked to stay. Just four takes, we're both extremely tense, afraid of hurting each other since the two slaps take place at the end of the shot, and the scene itself is very tense, with Vincent inarticulate, pale, violent. My hands are clammy, I'm cold. Régis is quite emotional. He loves filming these scenes, the crucial ones, the ones that make us nervous, the crunch points set out in the screenplay – the meeting, the tango, the row, Poulo Condor, the birth, the Perfume River. He's kept it all.

Perhaps the main danger now is this feeling of well-being, everyone's joy at shooting this film, we're getting comfortable. I sometimes worry about the pace, not only of the shoot but within the scenes as well. It's important to stay rigorous, and Régis does seem so happy with what he's doing that the lack of tension could be disastrous. But then at least one can mention this to him; he's open to any feedback.

Wednesday 26 June
A rather mixed day and evening. Continuity shots for the slap late evening. Naturally, we ran over time. The last close-up was on Linh Dan. To top it all I got a mosquito bite just below my eye. The couples look superb, their hair beautifully done, 1930s dresses, though tomorrow *Studio*[1] journalist Jean-Pierre Lavoignat and the guy

1 French film magazine.

filming the 'making of' documentary will replace the missing extras who, being amateurs, are no longer available! I start to get impatient about the rushes, and the production team worry about the delays and us running a week behind schedule. Régis shows me a letter from the completion bond insurers, requiring that we finish by 20 July, and perhaps even make up lost time, maybe there *is* a lack of pace?! This should be brought up with Régis. The technical and electrics people will love that! Threat of a late-afternoon storm. It's raining lower down, on Georgetown, which is shrouded in mist. No wind on the hill, brownish-yellow light, lightning, but luckily only a few drops of rain, which don't prevent us from filming the last shot: Vincent's arrival followed by the full moon.

Friday 28 June
Woken too early by Chiara[1] in tears, calling from Rome, worried about Marcello's operation, afraid that he's never going to wake up from it. I reassure her, at least I think I do, but it really disturbs me, can't get back to sleep, it's 7.30, oh well. Go through my usual routine, calmly, but my stomach is churning for the first time since I left – Paris and normal life flooding back a bit too suddenly, or perhaps I've forgotten too much, buried it all: I'm not ready yet. So, before eating, I do the clay-mask ritual, shower, then freshly squeezed mandarin juice from fruit bought at the market, coffee, toast, honey, music – Marvin Gaye – a bit of gentle tidying up, but none of it calms me down. The weather is gloomy when I arrive at the shoot, the grim business of moving set, taking down all the equipment. They'll probably have to work through the night. It's almost like the end of a shoot. The dinner

1 The author's daughter with Marcello Mastroianni.

scene before Linh Dan's confession, cutaway shots – necessary, but as Régis says, 'posing no particular challenge'. Film the kite scene; a big balloon is serving as counterweight, suddenly an eagle flies straight towards it, ready to pounce! Forty porters to load all the equipment, because tomorrow we'll be returning to the plantation, it's worse than climbing Mount Everest. Team photo at six this evening.

Saturday 29 June
Last day filming at Eliane's house, very cloudy, no team photo – a farewell drink instead. Just manage the final shot under a sulphurous sky, two takes, hill obscured by a white cloud which drifts right into this tropical house, monsoon rain.

Monday 1 July
Back to the factory. Three costume changes, because we're at the end now. Continuity shots from last week: the nosebleed, a wide shot, then the end of the fire scene with my father. We film this shot early, it's short, I have to cry, I find it really hard, frustrating to have to keep going back to the beginning, so quickly; I need three takes.

The dog has given birth to eight adorable puppies. I track them down under the house, little velvet playthings! A shot with Linh Dan, before Yvette's departure, very straightforward, and then it's time to wait. We're supposed to do the final shot with my father in the factory, but I can't imagine where I'll stand. Régis comes into make-up, preoccupied as usual, he suggests the rubber plantation, the house or even a makeshift shelter; I jump at the chance because it evokes childhood, love, cabins and also Jean-Baptiste. Jump right into the Rover with him, astounded, and concerned about the lack of light, it's already 4 p.m. and the rubber trees are hard to get to, and they gobble up light! Once we arrive at the house, I even go up to the first floor, telling Régis it's a pity we don't have a crane! From up there you can see the rubber trees gently climbing the hill, but the floor is fragile. You'd have to shore it up from underneath; the grips even start measuring up. We abandon that plan to stop the light from beating us, though we do manage an integral shot between the pillars, with the camera surrounded by white reflectors to cast as much light as possible, as we can't get a generator up there. Four takes, a single shot. I'm glad to have filmed there, pleased with this last-minute change.

Monday. Last day at the factory. I suggest to Régis that we do a shot from the middle of the rubber plantation, for possible inclusion in the second part. He agrees because all that actually remains for me to shoot is the scene where I meet Jean-Baptiste in the plantation. Better than I could have hoped. The rubber tappers with their head lamps, the drizzly morning mist, me in my boots tapping a tree myself, romantic wide shot and sneaky close-up, lit by the coolie's candle, the fine rain starting. This will be the last shot we get out of this serene, captivating, carefully planted place, with its scraped bark and the little bowls for collecting the tapped 'milk'. It gets spoilt by the rain, and then they make it into what they call 'craf': lower-grade rubber for tyre manufacture. The sum of French greed in these little bowls, this wealth that drips gently as honey, justifying our considerable presence here, come what may. These days, rubber tapping has almost fallen into abeyance, replaced by the more profitable harvesting of palm oil. Rubber has practically no role to play in our time.

Tuesday 2 July
Filming on the Ipoh road. Very typical village, with an old Chinese house surrounded by a courtyard. The kitchens have been renovated for the film – scullery, houseplants, birdcage, wonderful wood-burning stove, enormous French jade-green lacquer Henri II-style sideboard. At the end of the day, we film the preparations for the Christmas meal. The table is stunningly beautiful and realistic – such extravagance again, pure luxury – Peking duck, cakes, purées, pork pies and thirty extras for a shot no more than a few seconds long. We finish at 8.30 p.m.! Then a screening of the first tape in Régis's room, number 827, on the little Sony, early scene at the house with Minh Tan, but it's a rough edit and over-exposed. I must say I would have liked to have seen the rushes earlier so I could correct various things – surely my voice isn't really that strange, I hope it's just the effect of the video tape.

Wednesday 3 July
Final shoot at Ipoh. The port. Three shots, theoretically. Jean-Baptiste's lead coffin waiting in a hangar surrounded by local dockers carting ice, vegetables and raw meat around . . . the heat and smell make me nauseous. I hadn't anticipated the shock of seeing the lead coffin. It really hit me. Difficult showing emotion for the close-up. It was the anniversary of Françoise's death just a few days ago. Yesterday was Pierre's birthday,[1] and my sister Sylvie told me that my niece Caroline is pregnant. Life goes on, and I'm so far away, sometimes I'd like to distance myself from this film that's taking too much of my attention, and step back into my own life a little, but where? Chiara and Pierre are going to the States. The holidays start on

1 Pierre Torreton, Chiara's partner.

Sunday, but here there's only the world of the film; luckily, it's as rich and full as an egg.

Thursday 4 July

Having done a few little errands, I'm driven to Ipoh at around 2 p.m. This evening I'll be shooting the first scene in the village that gets burnt down, two days – or rather nights – of filming, my long scene with Guy ending with the village on fire all around us!

Once again, the set is stunning, a re-creation of Vietnam. Rainy, especially late afternoon: the ground is sodden. Luckily, I'm wearing my canvas lace-up boots. The first night isn't too bad, it's not cold and then I take half a sleeping pill to make sure I get seven hours' sleep. The second night I'm getting ready at about 5 p.m., still at the hotel, when I notice threatening clouds blowing towards us. I set off in the pouring, relentless rain. They've only managed to film the afternoon shot, which they were meant to do much earlier, with five minutes to spare! They've been waiting hopefully under their umbrellas as darkness has fallen, night shoot severely threatened, rain pouring down, serious risk of short-circuiting, and anyway, the lamps will never hold out.

When we get to the canteen at 9 p.m. it's horrible; empty beer and coke cans all over the tables, and supper as usual is lukewarm, greasy and repetitive – fritters, rice, fried chicken. The Malaysians are as fatty as their food! Well, not the technicians on this shoot. I'm told that Régis is resting. I'm sure he's trying to relax, we've got to wait, you never know, in theory, the shoot is supposed to stop at around 2 a.m. Not very likely.

The rain stops around midnight; they start testing the electrics, a decision has to be taken as we'll only be able to do half the scene, the long tracking shot with two cameras. Régis asks us to work over schedule and offers us a half day on Saturday. Everyone agrees, and we take up the challenge – because you have to gear yourself up again, I'd stopped thinking we were going to shoot tonight, and anyway midnight is often a big psychological hurdle. In the end, the shoot doesn't take long because the village burns pretty fast. The heat and smoke are overwhelming but, like the rain, they are living elements: annoying but also stimulating. I have more trouble than I'd anticipated with my lines, although I know them perfectly; it's the tension and I can scarcely breathe. Maybe weariness too – we finish at 4 a.m. And Erik Orsenna's script is often rather tricksy, a particular challenge when it has to be almost shouted. Régis tells me he noticed Dominique had the same problem during her long tirade as she leaves the factory. A two-camera scene. The close-up camera will film from a different angle for the final two takes. I've run out of ideas, there are too many variables outside my control for me to know how the scene will actually look. It's beautiful, incandescent. At the end, I have to run to safety between two houses. I can't do it for the last take because the fire has got so fierce, and the thatched roofs are scattering burning cinders everywhere, it's dangerous. But we have firemen on hand, ready to intervene. Tired, smoky, take a shower, light sleeping pill, the lovely, satisfying feeling of physical exhaustion. I end up sleeping till noon, waiting for Bertrand to arrive in the afternoon.

Saturday evening, 6 July
Shoot in the Chinese streets of Cholon, a totally outdoor set, rickshaws, street stalls, Chinese doors, incense, mystery and sensuality. I'm wearing a dark-blue dress, Guy and I are walking in front of the cart for a long,

twenty-five-metre tracking shot. My pace doesn't quite fit that of the dolly. I ask Régis to add a metre of rail at the front, but he doesn't have any left. In the end, we start with a static shot, to make sure we can finish in the doorway where Guy lies to me about his search for Camille. The set smells of freshly cut wood and incense. The weather is quite muggy, but as promised, we film for four hours.

Monday 8 July
Continental Hotel, Sheikh Adam Street, sixty-second day of filming. An authentic studio set, superb façade with balcony, striped cane pedestal tables, a real all-concealing trompe l'oeil, a white building transformed into the Bank of Indochina. Very noisy, which worries me, I can't help mentioning the noise to Régis, who says, 'Yes, perhaps, but it's so beautiful.' Fair enough, that was clumsy of me. But there is a real building site going up. This morning, they were shooting a scene in Cholon market and the generator broke down after the first take, two hours' delay. So I won't be filming that first scene where Guy asks me to marry him.

This evening was very tense, Eric Heumann is extremely concerned: the completion bond people are threatening to turn up. Bertrand tells me that once I've read it, a fax must be sent, suggesting strategies for catching-up on lost time. They can't get hold of a boat for my departure scene – the only steamship in Hanoi is being used by the crew of *The Lover*, and they've negotiated exclusive use. Régis agrees on a plane departure, to be filmed in Paris, as long as they don't deny him the boat scenes in Switzerland. I think he's right. The fax is too late and I'm told that 'they' are going to arrive. I can't think what's going to happen. Semi-private screening at

Régis's place, but on a big screen at last. The light is stunning and I find the scenes rather beautiful – a gunboat departure, the sampan, it's just a shame we couldn't see it earlier!

Tuesday 9 July

I'm filming early afternoon. Sense a great deal of tension, this morning's shoot was spoilt by noise from the building site. Eric Heumann paid the labourers to stop work for a few minutes while they did the takes. As soon as I arrive on set, I can feel that Régis is tense, very tense, smiling at Jean Yanne's jokes as he rehearses in a completely deadpan way, when the scene in fact demands a lot of passion. But very soon everything gets out of hand, I ask for real champagne that doesn't look like urine and has some bubbles in it, there are only two bottles; they have to 'make' more from apple juice. Then there's Jean's outfit, and also mine, which Régis doesn't seem to like, saying he needs to see an alternative. I hadn't realised that all this hadn't been sorted out with Gabriella. I tell him that I'm always ready two and a half hours early, and that if there's any uncertainty, it would be better if we could resolve it before I come on set. I suggest wearing the jacket, but he's upset and stubborn, and refuses, taking me up on trifling issues with the script. When I ask him what he thinks of the first take, he says he doesn't know any more, that he's been totally thrown off by a whole number of things. I stand up, asking that we take a pause so I can have a moment with him alone. There's no possibility of improvement when you're upset during a shoot. And I can see he's on the verge of tears, he's exhausted (on Sunday there was a six-hour meeting about making up lost time), and ever since our first day's filming in Malaysia, he's been under great pressure about delays due to technical problems. But most importantly, there are rumours going round in Paris that the delays are due to indecisiveness on his part. He's only made three films, which makes it easy for people to think that way. A mixture of pride and perfectionism is driving him to the end of his tether. I suggest that Jean wear his white Shantung suit – not only does it look better on him, but it's the marriage proposal scene. I can also sense that Régis hasn't quite nailed the scene, and knows it; we decide to start again, with different gestures, the ones Régis wants for this proposal, namely Jean grabbing hold of my hands and squeezing them tightly in his. After all the jokes and ridicule, the scene had lost a lot of its passion and impact.

In the end, it took us three hours to shoot, but we had such a lot to deal with – the noise, the five o'clock calls to prayer, me knocking over my glass of champagne during Jean's shot! And him, during mine, not managing to open the bottle – when it happened for the second time I asked them not to cut, and we popped the cork together and carried on with the scene, but then, twice, I stumbled over my words. I'd love to see their faces in Paris when they watch that take – it could feature in a collection of real howlers! And Jean's eyes, so intense and despairing, but how he loves to laugh and make people laugh.

This evening, our first screening in the ballroom, on the big screen. Louis Gardel, who has just arrived, can't believe it; I remind him that this is our first proper screening of the rushes, for the whole team, since we started shooting! Catonné's cinematography is beautiful and soft. Of course, the wide shots lose a bit of their impact with the TV format, but you get an idea of the scenes. In the final analysis, a lot of very writerly scenes, no transitional scenes, extremely subtle, a written rather than spoken language, as Régis wished, and appropriate for the era; the right balance between reality, realism and perfect words and gestures does demand almost constant vigilance. But I'm happy, I've got a real sense of our film and of everyone involved in *Indochine*.

A special day, full of challenges but also rewards. Just now Régis thanked me for being so positive! It's 1 a.m., time to sleep.

Wednesday 10 July

Continental Hotel. The shot where I rush in by car after Jean-Baptiste dies. I'm devastated when I see the new baby, he looks nothing like the gorgeous little Buddha we used in Penang – his hair is so dark. I suggest that we cut it as short as possible while he sucks on his bottle, under Cris's horrified gaze! In any case, I'd decided to wrap him in my white jacket, I'll just have to do it more quickly and hide him better. Late lunch with Bertrand, who wants to explain the situation and warn me how serious it is, without making me too concerned about the arrival of Mr 'Completion Bond' Garçon, whom I meet at the hotel – he's got that expert-accountant solemnity. He immediately starts telling me about the 'intelligent' solution of replacing the steamship scene with an aeroplane departure. I reply sharply that it's actually an economic solution, but that we did need one, and there's no ship. But mostly I try to persuade Eric not to bring him on set since he's only arrived today and must be tired. I know they're filming the scene of Dominique Blanc with her charming husband Raymond in one integral shot. I just don't think it's a good idea. They decide to visit the beautiful Continental Hotel set instead.

Bertrand and I chat for ages, freely, we trust each other

and know each other well. About Artmedia[1] in general, about the development of production in France, which even though I don't have much to do with it is still a crucial aspect of the whole process, and Artmedia are increasingly involving actors in the editing. He's more hopeful than me about the relationships between cinema, television and power. But you can't deny that fewer and fewer films are successful. Given that *The Lover* and *Indochine* are coming out almost simultaneously, I do hope they'll design the launch carefully. Eric Heumann is complex, and a manic depressive, and he's doing a lot of projects for just one man, including this huge film! But he's very bold and that's so unusual. If only he could buy back the completion bond!

Friday 12 July
Regatta. The bridge and the pale wood structures have been built from scratch by the crew – even the blue and white pavilion where we'll be shooting tomorrow, quite incredible. The extras look fantastic, their make-up and hair perfect. I wish Gabriella could have been here to see her wonderful outfits on this set. The river is wide and the surface current is strong. Huge trees sprawl close together on each bank, with their roots in the water and creepers and parasitic ferns hanging on to them like strange beasts. The light is both gentle and bright, the sky very hazy, not a breath of wind, the same suffocating heat as in the factory. Luckily, my white chiffon dress with the black polka dots is quite flimsy, and my white hat sufficiently large to hide my sodden nape, yet summery enough to allow in the light and what breeze there is. We shoot fast, often with two cameras, lots of footage, the

1 French production house.

start and finish of the race, the Admiral, Yvette in her red poppy-print dress. Dominique is finishing today, I can tell she's a bit disconcerted by how quickly we've shot; we haven't rehearsed much. She wears her dress, sunglasses and straw hat for the whole day, and the three of us take lots of photos. This is her last day!

Régis is very nervous, shouting a lot. Naturally, his assistant Jacques bears the brunt of it, but what's really bothering him is Eric (looking more and more depressed) and Mr Garçon sitting motionless on the bank watching these fierce outbursts. I think his agitation is largely due to their overly inert presence – they don't move, they don't leave each other's side and I even notice Eric walking towards the Italian restaurant with him. Vincent arrived here in a great rush, uncomfortable in his too-tight rowing outfit, because Régis wanted him to do more rowing practice before the shoot, and it seems that things got rather heated. The responsibilities are unending – what a breeze it is being an actor!

Saturday 13 July
Gardel and Nolot made their debuts today as planters in the blue and white pavilion; they were scared to death. In the background were the bridge, the extras (pale women in exquisite outfits), the boats going past ... it all looked beautiful, evoking that 'end-of-an-era' feeling. This is the beginning of the film. Horribly hot in spite of the enormous river, the biggest on the island, I think; it's like being back in Vietnam.

The food is mediocre, I hope they're going to make an effort tonight for the 14 July party that Vincent and I are organising in the gardens of the crew's house. As promised, Dominique has brought Chinese lanterns, and Guillaume is taking care of the music. The party ends with a downpour at about four in the morning. I wore white, with my red Bakelite cross: we'd asked everyone to wear only our national colours – red, white and blue. Régis dubbed me 'Red Cross'. As soon as he let go of his disapproval about the reason for the party, he had a good time, dancing, drinking whisky and Coke, with his bright-blue eyes and scathing sense of humour!

Monday 15 July
The rowing race. I'm not filming. In the evening, the team from Hong Kong, made up of businessmen, throws a noisy dinner to thank Régis for the holiday they've spent with us this week. Rowing is beautiful to watch and very strenuous, it's fierce and all-encompassing. The night finishes late, with beer – they're English – in the hotel nightclub.

Wednesday 17 July
Batu Gajah village. Same set we used for the daytime shots on the streets of Cholon, the child throwing a clod of earth at me at Kamjun Pisang. I fear it looks too static, the street around the child too quiet, but in this heat I'm unable to suggest another solution, have to admit we're on autopilot, shooting these scenes very fast. You don't always have time to think! This no-man's-land set reminds me of Almeria, amazing sets transported to hot, desert regions – just to be sure of dry weather?

Sunday 21 July
Arrival shots at Emile's house, a dilapidated yet mysterious and beautiful wooden mansion, complete with stone pillars and presided over by a magnificent tree. It's still stormy and hot. This evening, their efforts to film the final shot of mild rain were disturbed by the rain

itself – the generator becomes dangerous in wet weather. They work an hour over schedule. The sky is purple: the rain will be very heavy.

Régis has positive news about the rushes. Bertrand had also sent me a fax about them. Good, it makes up for the stress of the delays. There'll be a video screening tomorrow, Monday the 22nd.

A few days off from shooting, had planned to go to Pangkor with Hubert Saint-Macary. We're kept here in Ipoh because of a car accident – not serious, luckily – so spend a few days around the chlorinated swimming pool; oh, to have holidayed in that turquoise sea which we've ended up missing completely! Penang, 'Pearl of the Orient'!

Tuesday 23 July

Visit them shooting Linh Dan's departure by rail after her engagement – this is her last day, there'll be drinks, and Régis is going to record a message and have it played over the loudspeaker that makes the train announcements.

Ipoh Station. Feels just like Vietnam with the extras and the huge set – probably one of our biggest outdoor sets, along with the port and Jean-Baptiste's coffin. The shoot finishes around noon, Vincent has brought his video camera, and all the extras hang around. Linh Dan is overwhelmed and bursts into tears from the surprise, and from the whole unique experience she's had with us. Amid the many tears and hysterical laughter – Régis's message is long and complimentary – we finally get a glass of champagne! Then lunch in the gorgeous 1940s hotel next to the station.

By afternoon it's drizzling, which is worrying – we're supposed to shoot half the final scene at the airport because that's what we all finally agreed (I'll leave Indo-china by plane, with my concluding scenes on Lake Geneva. The decision was made easier by the small issue of the last scene in *The Lover* also being departure by steamship!). But the painted hangar, the Delage[1] and a few extras weren't enough to make Régis forget the inadequacy of the set for this pre-concluding scene. He decided to abandon and shoot the whole scene at La Ferté-Alais in France, where we had been going to simply finish off the aeroplane shots. He did well to stop, it wasn't right. I'm sure Labadie,[2] all dressed up as an extra, agreed, although he didn't quite come out and say so. So all in all, a kiss for Linh Dan this morning, and at about 5.45 p.m., my hand included in a continuity shot for the scene where little Etienne is eating an ice cream at the country club. That's film for you! It's still raining.

Wednesday 24 July
Make a start on the central scene – the rain, the car, the break-up – it's scheduled to take two nights. I can feel us sinking into night-weariness like quicksand. Unbelievably muggy, the padded car absorbs the heat like a sponge, only to leech it back on to us under the effect of the spotlights. Suffocating. Vincent crammed into a suit. Régis has shown me the storyboard. There are twenty-odd shots; in over an hour, we've done five.

Thursday 25 July
Régis wants to capture the essence of the scene, and at the same time, he's impatient to finish it (it wasn't in the storyboard anyway). Vincent very uncomfortable in his jacket. The very precise positions, the lack of space and

1 Glamorous car.
2 Jean Labadie, producer.

the intrusiveness of the camera render each take more and more unbearable. It's like an oven, we're drenched, awkward, and there's practically nothing we can do about it – the shots are short. I can tell Régis is very tense. The evening goes on and on with no end in sight. In any case, I urge him not to try to finish it tonight. We're no longer in a fit state!

Friday 26 July
The final night, full moon. We're less tired too, despite the disruption to our sleep patterns. I'm relieved that we can tackle the end of the scene rested, after a breather. We could never have done it as fast and as instinctively as this yesterday after the evening we'd had. A long integral shot of the two of us in the car, Vincent sitting on the floor with his head in my lap. Once again, Régis resists the temptation to shoot two separate close-ups. You can see us both reaching for each other without making eye contact; it's much more powerful shot together. A surreal sight, the fake rain through the projection rays, perfectly visible, standing out, and the full moon, not obscured by a single cloud from this artificial storm, like a Magritte. 1 a.m. I know that Régis has suggested a drink before he leaves for Penang tomorrow to shoot the last few scenes in Malaysia.

Sunday 28 July
Penang–Bangkok–Paris. Take a sleeping bill in Bangkok for the twelve-hour flight. I'm already a little uptight. Arrive Copenhagen around 7 a.m. for a breakfast stopover, we buy salmon, I loiter a bit longer than the others ... when I get to the gate, the plane is taxiing, with my luggage in the hold and my handbag on the seat. I'm speechless, staggered, thankfully holding my passport,

but with no ticket or money, only this huge salmon. Air France agrees to put me on another flight. Arriving home after four months carrying only a passport and a salmon – pretty casual and jet-set – I head back home to Place Saint-Sulpice after buying flowers in the Avenue Marceau, as if I'd simply popped out to the shops.

Cannes Festival

1994

Jury:
Clint Eastwood, actor (president)
Catherine Deneuve, actress (vice-
president)
Alan Terzian, producer
Alexander Kaidanovski, director
Gillermo Cabrera Infante, writer
Kazuo Ishiguro, writer
Lalo Schifrin, composer
Marie-Françoise Leclère, journalist
Pupi Avati, director
Sang Ok Shin, director

Cannes, Sunday

First meeting. Large, rather drab office. Clint Eastwood has me speak first, I seize the bull by the horns, but I can feel myself blushing! The meeting is quite long, an hour and a half by the time each of us has given our critique of six different films, plus the interpreting into Russian, Chinese and English. Many surprises, and it's also helpful for getting to know one another, chatting and learning about each other's tastes, because we're a cosmopolitan group of people. Though actually, despite the different worlds we come from, we seem in the main to have fairly similar views. We all adore cinema.

The table is so enormous that, presiding over it with Clint, I have to put on my glasses to be able to see him! Pupi Avati on my left, adorable, warm and humorous.

Delicious dinner. Quick trip to the Majestic Hotel to say hello to Gérard Depardieu and Roman Polanski. They're all in dinner jackets, feel rather uneasy with everyone looking at me and the tension palpable in the air, it's natural, but still, I think I'll avoid public spaces after the official screenings.

Gérard has lost weight. He was enormous in the film (Tornatore's *A Pure Formality*), but his great bulk was rather moving. That first scene where he's all white and naked under the shower was quite shocking, but not embarrassing. Big fat man with blunt-cut hair. Being heavy works for him, it makes you worry that he might explode, or hurt people when he gets angry, or injure himself. It's overwhelming, seems somehow suicidal. A time bomb waiting to go off, reminds me of

The Wages of Fear. And always that magnificent, musical voice.

Monday

We have a box with a private entrance and breakfast for those attending the 8.30 screening! I'll never make it! But I do, we slip in, I don't have to prepare anything, just arrive awake, and then leave straight through the wings and on to the CanalPlus boat for a quiet lunch. I like this, especially when there aren't any other official duties.

Three Colours: Red: visually stunning, serious, a bit slow, Jean-Louis Trintignant is superb. Very moving.

The Browning Version: extremely English, rather conventional, perfectly shot but the main thing is Albert Finney's masterly acting.

Cerruti's dinner in honour of Clint at the Moulin de Verger. Sat next to him, and the table was big enough and the dinner long enough for some private conversations, so I briefly, and lightly I hope, brought up the subject of *The Bridges of Madison County.* Jeanne Moreau was ravishing, subtle and intelligent. Back too late.

Exhausted this morning! Everything a bit rushed because there's an official lunch with the mayor, so we have to get all dressed up. In a nutshell, *The Whores*: black and white film, gorgeous to look at but not much in the way of plot. This afternoon, Iranian director Abbas Kiarostami's *Through the Olive Trees*, all about a film shoot, rather laboured but terribly sensitive and with magnificent panoramic shots.

Lightning trip home before the *Vivre!* screening. A (naughty) coffee to wake me up; the film is two hours long. I don't want to seem jaded, but really, at the end of a week, however you feel about the films, having to be here time and time again is a bit much. I prefer the daytime screenings. Getting to know the Palais very well. *Vivre!* is a wonderful saga, rich in family and historical detail, moving and very sentimental, the actors are fantastic. Impressive, with some remarkable scenes. It will have a wide appeal. I was extremely moved in a number of places. Standing ovation for this breath of fresh air.

'Every person has their own reason for being in the wrong. This means we need not judge, and so are freer to love.' Kontchalovsky.

Wednesday

Finally got to sleep at 3 a.m. My visible sleep deprivation would have been ample pretext for not turning up until the eleven o'clock screening, but against all odds, I decide to see *Dead Tired* at 8.30 a.m., so I can have a 'free' evening with no official duties. Hard work but possible. My eyes hurt, drink a coffee at the Palais. It's been raining a lot; you'd almost think you were in Brittany. Hardly anyone there, how gorgeous. Just a few movie buffs and passers-by asking for tickets without much hope of getting them. A fun session (the actors present, a comedy, Cannes, the festival – all the right ingredients for a rowdy audience). There's been a good buzz about this film. I'm curious. A very good debut, Carole Bouquet is stunning, and funny, but the weaknesses in the script become apparent after three-quarters of an hour, even though the film is quite short. Neither surreal nor realistic enough, and there are no sudden shifts or real tension, but I agree that the end works well – it's original and poignant.

Lunch on the *Don Juan* before the short films (hilarious, ironic black comedy from New Zealand). Then a meeting at the Carlton Hotel, which starts very slowly, but luckily, picks up once we start to repeat each other as we're all talking about the same films. The jury agrees a great deal, we're through to the second half of the festival and there hasn't yet been anything really stunning, or even terribly surprising. We'll probably have to tighten the noose on Saturday so that on Monday, we can discuss a few films in proper depth. But the culling will be harsh, with only seven prizes for twenty-four films! Clint suggests to me that we hold the discussions in his villa: it's bound to be more friendly that way. I agree that it will be easier just between ourselves – even the presence of the jury's press attaché bothers me and isn't necessary now that we all know each other.

At the end of the morning, a very long film called *Barnabo of the Mountains*, extremely long, extremely slow, very beautiful but what a lot to ask of your audience. But then maybe that's unfair: the shots are strong, it's a good story, and I'm sure Dino Buzzati's novel is wonderful, but so much waiting ... not an easy subject to turn into a film.

Thursday

Very short lunch break, I'm tired, take a nap to regain my strength. Tonight's film, *Dear Diary* by Nanni Moretti, is absolutely enchanting, serious, funny, very simple, rigorous and completely original. Although I did think that it wasn't really a movie, yet not quite a documentary either; no, it's a personal, intimate film. Totally unique.

Meet the *Guignols* crew. I did a short skit with them for *Nulle part ailleurs:*[1] very short and, I think, too realistic – Gildas had to state that I was a 'consenting victim', so it can't have been obvious or off-beat enough. Yesterday morning, I received a stunning bouquet of flowers with the message 'We're sure you have a microwave so we're

1 *Les Guignols de l'info* and *Nulle part ailleurs* are both satirical programmes on French TV.

giving you flowers instead.' This morning, on my way to breakfast at 10 a.m., I stumble over a huge parcel in the doorway. I guess it's from the Guignols: yes, a microwave! Pretty funny.

The Cambodian film, paddy fields, two hours long, a beautiful subject but again, very slow. In a lot of pain today, my head and throat are both agony. Hard work because my eyes are stinging (damned air-conditioning). I've hardly set foot outside, my shoes can't have been getting any wear at all ... hotel, car, Palais, boat, hotel, car, Palais, sleep, but too late at night!

Quick lunch before Eric Rochant's *The Patriots*. Very well done, nice camerawork, good performances from all the actors. Fairly classic, but it all works, and you're really interested in what's going to happen, for the whole two hours. But how much will one retain?

I haven't fallen in love with anything yet, not even the Nanni Moretti (though I do feel very fond of it). Only four more films. At Sunday's meeting I think we'll have to make some preliminary decisions before the debate, because so far we haven't ruled out anything, at least not in our joint discussions. This morning, Clint and I had another talk about Gilles Jacob's[1] possible presence at the Monday meeting. Why? In case we change our minds before Monday evening – but then why this secrecy, this complete silence around our discussions, if they're going to tell outside agencies in advance anyway?! What's the point of these contradictory measures? I'll have to bring it up tomorrow.

Saturday
A more disjointed day today, because I'm going to see the Tarantino film this evening. Mikhalkov's *Burnt by*

1 Festival director.

the Sun: beautiful film, very Chekhovian, real characters and wonderful directing, set in the Stalinist era. Harsh and very moving.

Late-afternoon jury meeting. We're pretty much in agreement, though I'm more in love with the Moretti than the others perhaps, and likewise for the Mikhalkov. Our differences will become clearer on Monday, when we will, sadly, have to do the eliminations. But I'm sure everyone will agree on tonight's Tarantino. The audience is won over before it even begins, we could almost be in New York it's so buzzy. Brilliant, original, with crazier characters than you could ever imagine. Violent, funny, fantastic directing. Dropped into the 'boys and girls' party in my white dress. He'd already left. A sandwich at the Gray with Jacques Wolfsohn, quick nightclub stop, it's 2 a.m. already!

Total exhaustion this morning – antibiotics plus the lack of sleep! The Indian film goes on for two and a half hours! And more than half of it in black and white. Catch myself nodding off several times: it's an ordeal. Half an hour for lunch, then *The Violin Player*; though not actually long, it seems interminable – a subject but no real script. Sadly, Richard Berry's technical performance is the only redeeming factor.

Long weekend, wonderful weather – Cannes is absolutely packed. Feel like going out even though I'm so tired, so Isabelle, Jean-Yves and I go to Häagen-Dazs, who gives a damn! At Port Canto we drink mineral water, which is a bit sad, but at least we get some fresh air. I've reached the end of my rope today, but perhaps that's because I know we're nearly finished. I've had enough; tomorrow it'll become evident that having to select and judge isn't my forte. I've managed not to think about it during the whole festival. Time to sleep.

Tristana

1969

Director: Luis Buñuel

Screenplay: Luis Buñuel and Julio Alejandro, adapted from the novel by Benito Pérez Galdós

Cast: Catherine Deneuve (Tristana), Fernando Rey (Don Lope), Franco Nero (Horacio), Lola Gaos (Saturna), Jesús Fernández (Saturno), Antonio Casas (Don Cosme), Sergio Mendizábal (the tutor), José Galvo (the bell-ringer)

Director of photography: José F. Aguayo

Costume designers: Rosa Garcia, Vicente Martínez

Additional music: Frédéric Chopin

Release date: 1970

Tuesday 28 September
First day of filming. 9 a.m. Blue skies, crisp, cold – I'm freezing in my brown crêpe de Chine suit, and also full of nerves, though not as bad as Fernando. The calm, organised feel of a crew who already seem used to each other, a real feeling that the film has properly started, surely and flawlessly. Buñuel warm and relaxed, like when I saw him in Madrid last week. He might look a bit glum but he doesn't miss a trick. Often he'll make discoveries while we're rehearsing, changing and improving things right up to the shoot. Likewise with the script – some very clear directions for the character of Don Lope, which he knows to the core. I don't remember Buñuel being so precise with his actors, but then I forget that this Spanish film is even more his than *Belle de Jour*, which was written eight years ago and still means so much to him.

Lunch break at 1 p.m. precisely. I can tell he keeps very regular hours and inflexible habits – if the work schedule gets done early, we stop. Afternoon: two shots in the church, Fernando a bit stiff, Buñuel isn't satisfied, he'd rather change something than make do with a faulty glance or movement. Being the only one filming in French makes me more confident about shooting in the midst of this big crew. Only the first assistant knows what I'm saying. Buñuel can't alter the script between takes. Finish at around 4.30 p.m.

Wednesday 29 September
Same set, same place, Fernando more relaxed. Buñuel takes me into the church to see the huge, recumbent,

alabaster statue that I have to lie down on later. It's a Berguette, remarkable. According to Buñuel, he's Spain's greatest sculptor. That scene was added once he'd visited the locations. He's excited to be shooting in Toledo, lots of childhood memories. He gets a kick out of explaining the end of the scene to me: Don Lope, confident that Tristana will have been moved and aroused by the statue, approaches her solemnly but with a questioning look in his eyes; putting on a stupid smile, she tells him to go shopping for slippers. The point is barely disguised – but then Buñuel likes to take the emotion out of serious moments, he prefers to avert his gaze. Likewise, he injects surrealism into the most classic, traditional scenes, for which he has little patience. I'm sure the film is going to be quite different from the screenplay. Each scene is changing form; he often shifts emphasis, accentuates and alters things during rehearsal.

Thursday 30 September
Important changes for me as we're shooting one of the film's final scenes. Heavily made up, pale, with doll-like pink cheeks, fingers dripping with rings, hair pulled back, I'm rather dreading Don Luis's reaction – in Madrid he was so impatient that we only did the briefest of costume fittings. He seems OK, then loses his temper because my artificial leg isn't up to scratch. Ten minutes later he's decided to direct differently so that today we'll only get a sense of the limp. I'd bound my ankle to help stiffen my weirdly shaped leg; Don Luis didn't like that, though he was happier once we'd draped it in brown silk. I find it hard to really embody the scene because of the major practical challenges – the dolly, as well as my limp, and having to concentrate hard on what the priest is saying as he's speaking in Spanish. Not very happy with the first

shot. The second part is seated, so that will help me to concentrate better.

Friday 1 October

Scene with Saturno the mute in the bedroom at the Quinta.[1] I know that Buñuel considers this scene crucially important: he's given it greater emphasis than in the screenplay and is altering it as we shoot. From the first shot, he transforms the implication that Tristana is being provocative into a fact, and then a habit. It's done in three parts: the mute Saturno comes in from the garden to Tristana's bedroom, where she's sitting at her dressing table. He approaches and lays a hand on her shoulder; after a few seconds, she shakes it off. He leaves; Tristana goes on to the balcony and pulls open her dressing gown as he watches, astounded, from the garden below. First rehearsal: when Saturno puts his hand on my shoulder, Buñuel tells me not to react straight away; the second time, he asks me to convey through gestures 'not today but maybe tomorrow'. The next scene is my wedding to Don Lope. I'm already smiling.

Monday 4 October

Still the same location because this scene has been cut into so many shots. Have to toss underwear on to my artificial leg lying on the bed, and it's a real challenge making the lace fall exactly on the shoed foot. Buñuel hates it when time gets wasted on location; if he could, he'd shoot everything in the studio.

Tuesday 5 October

Scene where Don Lope astonishes Tristana by helping a

1 Spanish country house.

93

thief: he sends the police in the wrong direction. Toledo, narrow streets and serious lighting issues despite the skill of the technical crew, who have hung sheets to soften the glaring sun; the grips scale houses at incredible speed, like monkeys. The thief is played by such an incompetent local boy that, for a moment, I think Buñuel is going to abandon the scene. But in the end, he gets round the problem to avoid incurring technical difficulties. It's very cold and my mourning dress doesn't offer much protection. In the evening, to my amazement, dinner at Don Luis's house. He tells me it's the first time for thirty years that he's socialised at night during a film shoot. We drink a little and laugh a lot, he's cheerful and chatty, telling coarse, funny stories about Mexico.

Wednesday 6 October
Shoot in the cathedral tower – we climb 150 steps to the platform housing the enormous bell which cracked all the windows in Toledo when it first rang, according to Buñuel. They had to change the clapper to ensure the safety of the tower itself – it was vibrating. At least twenty feet across. Buñuel offered 100,000 pesetas to anyone who could tell him how the bell had been hoisted to the top of the tower. Difficult shoot, such a confined space; filming the shot where I see Don Lope's head hanging from the clapper. The make-up artist was working on the amazing wax head until two o'clock this morning, which is there, swinging gently, held up by invisible thread. My two deaf-mute colleagues make me laugh, but their incompetence gets on Buñuel's nerves; he teases them a little harshly. One has serious acting ambitions and wants to change his name from Jesús Fernández to Jesús Hamlet. When he started talking about his character's psychology, Buñuel made him re-read the script. I was

laughing: it reminded me of yesterday when we were shooting and Buñuel enigmatically told me, 'Above all, spare us the psychology.' It was the shot where I watched Saturno as I flashed my dressing gown on the balcony.

Thursday 7 October
Damp, cold, grey skies. We shoot in the garden for the first time, a stroll during which Lope, feeling Tristana distancing herself, speaks the fantastic line: 'I'm your father and your husband, and I'll alternate between the two as I please.' Buñuel gives Fernando specific guidance on the way he looks at me; it should be suspicious and hypocritical. The run-through is better than the actual take, but he accepts it. I'm aware of the need to be as consistent as possible – he knows the outlines of my script but doesn't follow it during the shoot, so he always keeps the first good take, not knowing if I've made mistakes; anyway, he'd never repeat it just for that.

Brilliant sunshine at around 2 p.m. Because the sky has changed so radically, we work up a shot where I've moved away from Lope to gaze at the Tage. Superb view – the river and some nearby ruins. The little bright-green crane intrinsic to almost all the shots is already in place. Buñuel wanted one for *Belle de Jour*, but they don't have them in France. He's told me how carefully he avoids the touristy side of Toledo, so, looking at this landscape enhanced by the height of the crane, I can't help teasing him by remarking how visually attractive the shot is. He laughs, muttering. Ten minutes later, he tells me he doesn't like 'obvious' shots and loathes it when you can sense the presence of the camera, so we're going to shoot the same thing but using a dolly and no background whatsoever. It makes me sad to see how constantly he questions himself, even when it's just prompted by a joke, as in this case.

During the hour's wait between the two shots, I come across a shy, timid, little black dog and cuddle it on my lap. When we come to shoot, Buñuel asks me to keep it in my arms. We laugh at how some people are bound to interpret this; it tickles him. I know he'll keep that shot rather than the first. I finish early, dissatisfied with my day's work and worried because I still haven't seen any of it on screen. I often feel as if I'm about to sit an exam when I come on set, knowing he might change everything round, giving very precise instructions, but not talking about it beforehand because he thinks that would be too fussy. Given that he's already told me how crazy Signoret drove him with her costume issues, I'm more hesitant than ever about pestering him ahead of time. I'm sometimes surprised at his choice of actors – many are conventional, classic, yet he still manages to 'break' their game and warp what they do with barely a word.

I feel alone.

Friday 8 October
It's raining today, for the first time. We all wait in the café until we can film our first shot, where I appear in the wheelchair. Buñuel is very impatient; I notice it's so extreme that he often says 'action' twice. His friend Barros, a famous surgeon, will be acting in this scene; his childlike excitement and awkwardness is touching – he's so keen to be in a film. Buñuel can't understand why, especially as we're surrounded by gaping onlookers. He asks me to say a few words in Spanish – he's added them at the last moment. Untranslatable into French because the coarse, insulting comment relates to a peculiarly Spanish notion. Carrière[1] will have to find a

---

1 Jean-Claude Carrière, frequent collaborator and screenwriter for Buñuel.

way. *Como esta la salud Tristana? Y la de su madre cómo va?*

We stop quite early because night is falling, although the scene isn't finished. Dinner with Buñuel at La Venta de los Aires restaurant. We drink a fair amount. Long silences because Don Luis is very sensitive to noise. Feels uncomfortable. Not that he notices – he's on great form. Tells us he's going to do a promotional film for Vichy Saint-Yorre, and he's been given total artistic licence. He's thinking of Christ on the cross with the Virgin Mary crying at his feet – he's offered a sponge soaked in Vichy Celestin water and, with a painful, awkward movement, motions 'no' with his hands, murmuring 'Saint-Yorre'. We burst out laughing. 10 p.m.

Saturday 9 October
Filming in an extraordinary forge that's been renovated especially for the film; Buñuel first saw it fifty years ago! The bevel is already in place. I'm constantly amazed by the efficiency of this crew. At 10.30 a.m. everything is ready. Three-minute shot, all the workers at their posts. I collapse just as we begin the second take – not sure whether it's the tension or the smell of coal. Buñuel sends me home until 2 p.m. He thanked me several times for suggesting that Saturna wear glasses (the actress has just had an operation and there's a very noticeable scar under her eye). I'm often stunned by how direct he is – he doesn't hide his feelings. So, when she arrived and he saw the scar, he didn't mince words or conceal his shock or annoyance: I don't think Saturna can have missed it!

Monday 8 November
Difficult start today. The scene where Saturna and I go for a walk, and I choose one of two streets. I'm so aware

of Buñuel's irritation and impatience with the slightest setback that I become completely paralysed. Even though this shot shouldn't be difficult, I can't seem to break it down. He settles for three takes. Grim lunch at La Venta de los Aires, I feel like crying. When a shot goes badly, I feel like a useless object. Totally useless, because my dialogue is of no interest to him, he's not even listening. This will be a proper Spanish film, I'll be dubbed, which I sometimes find hard to accept. One shot this afternoon, a bit better. My first really bad day.

Saturday 13 November
Two very brief shots. My first encounter with the painter. Buñuel seems to be hesitating a lot – I'm sure there'll be a few major changes by Monday. He needs the weekend to rework the scene. Shooting finished by 3 p.m. They were only auxiliary scenes.

Monday 15 November
It's never been as cold as this. Get to know Franco Nero, he's open, friendly, informal. Hard for a Latin man to fully accept the actor's position in life. Every time Buñuel gives precise instructions for our meeting and first contact, his delicacy makes him pull back and he erases the few words he's just added. Like him, I favour a lack of precision for this crucial meeting, don't want to know exactly what he's told him to say, for once, rather than express physically. My throat hurts. Luckily, I'm not filming tomorrow. Buñuel tells me the wedding scene will be as harsh as I can possibly imagine; when I ask about colour, he tells me to let the cameraman and laboratory worry about that: he's delegated those concerns definitively now. Pity. For the first time, I'm conscious of his

age – probably because I've never seen him relinquish something from weariness before.

Tuesday 16 November
Flu. Stay in bed all day. Lots of vitamin C.

Wednesday 17 November
I'm made up very pale, which makes me feel more comfortable – the further I am from myself the bolder I feel, and anyway, although disturbing, it's not ugly. Everyone thinks I look evil. Scene where we leave the church in the snow, I'm lifted into the wheelchair like a doll, kept nice and warm under the blanket. The snow machines aren't very good, and Buñuel decides to do without them. I'll always be staggered by his impatience, and particularly his punctuality – even when it counts against him. At 12.50 he says he'll be stopping in ten minutes. The shot isn't even nearly right, the first takes are poor, with five minutes left to go, one of the actors can't get his words out, too bad, we finish at one. I'm stunned. We redo the shoot differently at the end of the day.

Friday 19 November
The film's first scene, on the esplanade. I went to bed early so Tristana would look well rested on her first appearance. Grey skies, fog, we only start filming at around 10.30. I hope we don't get delayed: I've got to leave for Paris tomorrow. Only two shots before lunch, we'll never get through it. I get more and more annoyed, drinking cognac in my trailer. In the end, there are three shots left for tomorrow.

Saturday 20 November
Despite the weather, we manage to get the three shots

done. We only do two for the afternoon scene in the station. Buñuel has changed how it ends: Don Lope has been hiding in the station, and finds Saturna there; she'd accompanied me. He tells her, 'She'll be back.' The most beautiful station I've ever seen, Arabic, Moorish, with stained-glass windows and synagogue-type columns. Rush off to Paris at about 4 p.m.

Wednesday 24 November
First night. I sense that Don Luis wants to make this relationship more and more platonic: my scenes with the painter are increasingly chaste. We film until 2 a.m. He's tired and jumpy.

Friday 26 November
First studio shoot, in the painter's studio. These scenes are more conventional, and more challenging.

Saturday 27 November
Same location. Luckily, this is the final day. I've visited the set for Don Lope's apartment, reminds me of *Repulsion*, a real apartment with rooms and a connecting corridor. The studio is tiny, like Twickenham, only two sets. We're going to start in the corridor on Monday, I think I'm going to like it, doesn't even feel like a set.

Monday 29 November
Inside Don Lope's office. Buñuel tells me, giggling, that he's plagiarising himself – I'm to drop a bottle, just like in *Belle de Jour*. Hairdressing problem – we have no coils, plaits instead, oh well. I like the slightly sordid décor. The cameraman really takes his time.

Tuesday 30 November
'Be really innocent,' Buñuel tells me with a little smile. I have fun caricaturing innocence during rehearsals. Problems with the dog, who's supposed to try and get into the bathroom where the mute man has locked himself in.

Wednesday 1 December
Dinner in the dining room. The scene is cut into a lot of short shots, it takes a long time, Buñuel gets impatient, starts furiously crumpling the tablecloth, rubbing the wine stains, moving the salad dressing. These scenes are so well prepared he can devote a lot of time to detail, sometimes even between takes, despite the protests of the continuity girl.

Thursday 2 December
Finish the dinner scene. He tells me they'll despise me in America for dipping soldiers into soft-boiled eggs.

Friday 3 December
Nightmare: the grotesque spectre of Lope in nightshirt and nightcap. In the evening, he asks us to re-film the scene tomorrow. The end wasn't clear enough – he's decided to return to Tristana's childhood via a memory linked to Don Lope, who would have looked so frightening to a child. The scene where Lope seduces me as I'm ironing in the sitting room: as clear and precise as I'd imagined.

Saturday 4 December
Second time frame. Lope suddenly unwell, old and decrepit. Don Luis compliments me on Tristana's hair and outfit for the first time – which makes me think it must have been not quite right before. Chickpeas for

lunch. Buñuel tells me about *The Sinners* again, that famous scene I'd forgotten where Romy Schneider poses a choice between two pellets of bread because 'Two things are never identical'. I ask my table-mates to choose one particular pea in the dish, but we all go for the same one!

Tuesday 7 December

The assistant director told me that a couple of the cameramen saw a screening of Friday's shoot and that they are the two best shots in the whole film. He picked up on how, in the bedroom, after taking off my dress, I undo my stockings. I wasn't asked to do that. I wanted to show Buñuel that I was quite happy in my underwear; before we even started rehearsals, he was convinced I was prudish. Even when I kept trying to reassure him that I wasn't. He would say, 'I'm about to cut, just a moment ...' He made Pierre, his assistant, tell me to speak more slowly from now on. That's the dubbing again!

Scene with Lope before our stroll. A note on my script indicated irony and arrogance. He asks me to be more submissive; when Pierre shows him the script, he tells me, laughing a little, 'We always write nonsense! And that's how you get contradictory scenes.' He's always thinking of changes, and often has the previous scene re-read to him at the very last moment. Because we haven't shot the film chronologically, I think he's trying not to spoil a strong scene that we've already shot by creating the same tone in an earlier one. Tristana and Lope's relationship deteriorates, and it's important that there's a gradual, steady shift in the balance of power between them. I hope these intentions, so clear and obvious when you read the script, will translate on to the screen. Laughing, I tell Buñuel how, in the corridor, I've been showing how relaxed I am by juggling with my hat while whistling.

He laughs and makes me do it on film too! We have to start the scene again because the hatstand behind Fernando makes it look as if two horns are coming out of his head. As it's the first time I cheat on him with the painter, according to Buñuel the symbolism would be glaring – well, for some critics, sure – so I put my hat on one of the horns to sidestep that misunderstanding.

Thursday 9 December
Argument with Lope, and that scene I love where he becomes humble and tender again, the long, semi-circular tracking shot reminds me of the railway. Don Luis makes a fuss because our hair is too shiny. He doesn't dare give me a hard time but asks the crew to put powdered milk on Saturna's hair. He's very concerned with realism, and the details of the plot, which surprises me, although I'm also pleased that he's taking such total ownership of this film – no one except him can really understand everything that has to happen in it. All these scenes are important, necessary. Never mere links – each one contributes to a character's psychological development. At the same time, this continual control exhausts him.

Friday 10 December
Casa Tristana. Lots of problems with the dog, two integral shots, he makes us put on headscarves because of the dust, and to hide our perfect hairdos. He doesn't encumber himself with pointless problems; if one shot isn't working technically after a couple of takes, he'll change it so as not to wear out the actors ... the risks he takes are those of someone who's seen it all. It's different with a younger director – risks often come from a lack of awareness. He knows exactly what he's risking, and does it anyway.

Saturday 11 December
Lunch at the bell-ringer's house. The Tiridiana beggar, his eyes are extraordinary, so shiny and protruding. It's quite a challenge to eat *migas* – a typical dish made with fried-bread croutons – while talking!

Monday 13 December
There were two shots left to do, in the tower staircase. When we don't finish a shot on a Saturday, there'll almost always be changes by Monday. This time, there's two new shots: in one of them the mute character lifts my skirt right up with a clothes-peg!

Tuesday 14 December
Tristana's return to Lope's apartment, completely different now, with a delightful bedroom. Three shots. Buñuel introduces me to the actor playing the doctor by saying how much he looks like a young André Breton. A bit depressed this evening, I don't always feel as if I'm being directed, yet at the same time, I haven't seen any rushes so I can't correct myself. Barros was on hand in case we needed advice on the doctor's movements and interventions. He dreams of being an actor when he's one of the most famous surgeons in Europe!

Wednesday 15 December
Scene with Horacio, piano, pre-recorded score, difficulties with the Chopin nocturne. Only one shot because we've re-filmed the scene with the bell-ringer. Don Luis doesn't treat his actors particularly gently; it's very frightening when he interrupts during a take.

Thursday 16 December
End of the scene with Horacio, hard going, Buñuel cuts

the end where Horacio carried me into the bedroom to make love. He's hesitant, asking our opinion for the first time. I prefer it this way, it'll only make the scene at the Quinta with Saturno more striking.

Friday 17 December
Lope's arrival. Everything goes slowly today, only one shot and it's 4 p.m. We've gone over it several times: I was sitting with one leg hidden underneath me, but when I stood up it kept poking out. Coming back after the wedding, Lope freshly bathed and in his pyjamas in the corridor, me sneering. I go into my room without him. Grim and terrifying. A few shots screened on Italian TV. I do an interview, I'm faltering and unsure, I'd better ask to see it first.

Saturday 18 December
Credits today. He's asked me to do my hair however I want, wear everyday clothes, he explains that he's shooting close-ups that he'll fade very simply into shots of Toledo. Franco and Fernando have already done it. He wants me like I was two months ago, the day of the costume fittings.

Monday 20 December
Learn of a new alteration when I arrive this morning: we're filming the two shots that will be edited into the priests' conversation and then Don Lope's death. Maybe tomorrow will be my last day. I don't know what induced him to change it at the last moment. With him, weekends always result in plenty of surprises! Problems with my artificial leg: it has to be fixed on, turning is disastrous, and we've rehearsed so much today that the crutches are hurting my armpits. He asks me to change my make-up

back to what I wore at the Quinta. When the assistant director objects, he replies that logic mustn't always take precedence over the rightness of something else that may have been less obvious at the beginning. Fernando has been in make-up for two hours, he looks like a mummy. We shoot the scene in the right order, and then backwards, without worrying too much about continuity, but the gradual build-up of anxiety, when reversed, produces an extraordinary effect. He keeps laughing. His compliment of the day, and it is one: 'You'd be great in a vampire film.' He likes my eyes heavily rimmed with kohl, keeps telling me I'm 'devilish'. As I go to open the window so the cold will kill off poor Lope, I'm reminded of the witch in *Snow White*. I can sense both worry and relief in Don Luis.

Tuesday 21 December
Last day. Alone on set. End of the scene in the office. Don Luis seems very reluctant to give me clear instructions. Every time he makes a suggestion, he quickly adds, 'But as you like, don't take any notice.' We do the scene backwards. Twice, because Aguayo, the cameraman, insists on changing the light – who does he think he is?! Last shot, in the bedroom, Lope's head in the bell, waking up, and then again in reverse. My last shot at the piano: leg folded underneath me, so my knee looks like a stump. I'll never forget that last image, perched a foot above the floor with the camera at ground level, and it seeming to me like the whole crew was looking up my skirt.

The April Fools
1968

Director: Stuart Rosenberg

Screenplay: Hal Dresner

Cast: Jack Lemmon (Howard Brubaker), Catherine Deneuve (Catherine Gunther), Peter Lawford (Ted Gunther), Myrna Loy (Grace Greenlaw), Charles Boyer (André Greenlaw), Jack Weston (Potter Shrader)

Director of photography: Michel Hugo

Costume designer: Donfeld

Music: Marvin Hamlisch

Release date: 1969

Travel to New York with my agent Giovanella Giannoni to shoot *The April Fools*. Escorted by CBS, who are producing the film; try to avoid them – just as I should have avoided Les Artistes Associés in St Tropez. I hate St Tropez, I always will, and I'm not too keen on the people who go there either. Having circled overhead for hours, we arrive in New York. It's hot and sticky, they give me red roses, I'm tired of all this waiting. An assistant calmly suggests that I try on my outfits with Donfeld, the costume designer – they're insane. I go to bed. I like the hotel drugstore and bar; they serve Italian coffee. My room is decorated à la *Madame Butterfly*, and I can see the park. Feel pretty good when I wake up, and decide to go shopping for tights before my first fitting. Bump into Giovanella on Fifth Avenue. The weather is really close and oppressive. The fittings are rather disappointing, the materials cheap. Donfeld is cold, stubborn and pretentious, and he won't let Stuart Rosenberg – the director – attend. I meet with Rosenberg, he's kind of puppyish, his eyes are sad and very kind. Nice lunch with Giovanella and Haussman, my American agent from W. Morris. I won't get to spend much time with my friends, I'm refusing interviews already, I feel tired and people are getting on my nerves. I would like to be morally strong and physically well for the film.

Giovanella and I decide to go to the movies, there's a lot showing, we choose Polanski's *Rosemary's Baby*. It's absolutely packed, the film has already started. In my opinion Roman ought to watch his taste for the bizarre. He always captures something important, but it's a bit too graphic. He deploys Mia Farrow well, by which I mean he also makes use of her shortcomings. It's rather similar to *Repulsion*. Later, we decide to have dinner, I take her to one of my favourite New York restaurants, an Irish place called P. J. Clark's. We have spinach and mushroom salads and hamburgers, she loves it. The heat and the Irish coffee make me tipsy. We head to Broadway, which is full of odd, obscene, obese people, even the young ones. We see *Fame*. The sound quality is terrible, and I struggle to understand the dialogue although the story flows well. It's good, a little superficial, but then I am too – I keep whispering with Giovanella. The second half is better, the audience loves it, especially the rather crass caricatures.

Saturday 20 July

Meeting with my director Rosenberg. He wants to rehearse, or at least make me feel that's what we're doing. We read, and he munches on sunflower seeds. He wants to see me again at 5 p.m., I'm furious. I go back to the hotel to rehearse with Jack Lemmon, he's charming, surprising; we read for forty-five minutes before going for lunch in the village with my agent. It's horribly hot; I've put my hair up in a big scarf to try and stay fresh, but it doesn't work for long. At the square we come across a very strange open-air show, a band and choirs of gaudily dressed, conservative young Americans singing charm-lessly about peace and equality, refusing to acknowledge their own racism.

Monday 22 July

Get up. Fittings today. Two crews. I speak to the head cameraman in French, no problem with the make-up, but the clothes aren't great. Horrendous migraine towards the end of the day, but I still have to do the publicity shots, they're merciless, though in the end, it doesn't take long. I can't move, we get the doctor over. Giovanella and my hairdresser Simone become impromptu nurses; they declare that I've got food poisoning from eating herrings!

Tuesday 23 July

Lunch with my agent at L'Etoile. No willpower, find it impossible to diet. Yesterday's upset completely forgotten. Big party at the St Regis this afternoon, all the snobs out from their ivory towers, I manage to smile and look relaxed for a couple of hours in my white Saint Laurent dress. Leave, exhausted, decide to walk to the hotel.

Shoot in Central Park. I can't stand the dresser. Go home in the Cadillac to avoid the fans. It's pouring, traffic at a standstill. Meet Frances from *Newsweek*, she's sympathetic and delightful.

Sunday 28 July

Lunch with Frances in the countryside. They almost don't let me in because I'm wearing trousers. It's delicious, and we chat easily, she's funny and a bit hysterical, I like her very much.

Monday 29 July

Dreadful costume fitting. I'm starting to think we should use Saint Laurent, and so are they. Donfeld is nervous and incompetent. Photo session with Jerry Shatzberg. Surprised to bump into Polanski, who persuades me into a drink at Sardi's, where we meet Warren Beatty – he's so smooth. Feeling rotten, relieved to have dinner with

Vadim – that indulgence of his which can so often seem weak is sometimes comforting.

Tuesday 30 July
See Peter Evens, who's writing an article on David Bailey; I'm friendly but guarded. More fittings, I'm demoralised, and then Stuart, the director, turns up; luckily, he's not impressed by the costumes either. All a bit bland.

Wednesday 31 July
Night shoot in Greenwich, Connecticut. Frances comes along. I wear Saint Laurent in the end, and feel relieved and comfortable. Donfeld, the costume designer, pulls a face. I couldn't care less.

Monday 5 August
Photo session with Jerry Shatzberg for the *Newsweek* cover. A bit nervous, but it goes well.

Saturday 10 August
See *Hair* after a three-week wait; the youth and passion of the troupe are so exhilarating. The lyrics are mediocre, but the songs and the way it's directed are fantastic. Americans don't mind making fun of themselves, for them it's a farce, but actually it's quite an accurate portrayal of a certain sector of teenage America.

Sunday 11 August
Leave for Los Angeles in my big yellow hat. I stopped in the Village on the way and almost missed the flight. The weather is gorgeous. When we land, I realise I've fallen asleep on my neighbour's shoulder. Move into a white house with a lovely heated swimming pool.

Monday 12 August
Great to see Agnès Varda and Jacques Demy. He's already been filming for eight weeks.[1]

Tuesday 13 August
Shoot in a baroque house with a green slate roof. Not much for me to do. Time drags.

Wednesday 14 August
Meet up with Pascal Thomas for an interview. Agnès Varda is doing an *Elle* photo shoot. In the end, they come to the house to do it. In the evening, we meet up with Jerry Shatzberg to see *The Producers*, a comedy about a Hitlerian musical intended to be a total flop, but that's actually a roaring success. Small budget, big ideas.

My hairdresser Simone told me she wanted to go back to Paris. I'm furious. She hates Los Angeles, stays in all the time. I'm so disappointed, angry, what a pain! Should I get someone else over from Paris? What about the production? More and more, I need time alone to relax, I'm finding people increasingly difficult, I miss my Françoise, feel her with me constantly, a source of both courage and sadness.

Saturday 17 August
My little man has arrived. I'm worried he's missed the flight, waiting, can't see him, getting annoyed – I've got to be at George Cukor's for dinner at seven – and then there he is, shy, tanned, holding his little Vuitton bag. The air hostess told me that all he would eat or drink was bread and milk. I'd bought a camera so I could get pictures from the moment he arrived. Simone put him to

1 *Model Shop*, with Anouk Aimée.

bed, and we left late for the dinner, it had already started. Cukor, Hepburn, everyone chatty and delightful, lovely house, very English, crammed with photos and souvenirs and paintings, a great evening, puts my mind at rest.

Sunday 18 August
Go over to Agnès and Jacques Demy's house for dinner, their parents are there, they talk of nothing but their film.

Sunday 25 August
To the Rosenbergs' – a pretty, well-decorated house, but I really don't have anything in common with him. Simone is driving me mad, carrying on as if nothing has happened. I know she's going to leave.

Tuesday 3 September
Jacques and Agnès come over for the birthday. My present hasn't arrived but there's champagne, it's very hot, the swimming pool looks as if it's steaming. Everyone swims.

Sunday 8 September
Agnès's place for dinner, rather tense evening because of the friction with Simone. I'm going to let her go. I've had enough, it's chilling to see how rude I've become, I don't care for her at all anymore.

Friday 13 September
It only sank in later. My baby Christian went back to Paris this evening, so we were at the airport. He was chatty and wide awake. As for Simone, she's leaving tomorrow morning, her face a picture of sorrow, I don't care, and anyway, I know someone's coming from Paris

to replace her, which makes me feel better. Coarse, drunk Americans, coarseness really bothers me. They don't know that I can hear them from behind this curtain. The vodka I drank before dinner made me tipsy. I finish late, not very proud of myself, I always think things are my fault. Simone is leaving. I think she was expecting to stay a little longer, thinking that at the last moment I would beg her to stay. No. Pettily, she drops a hint about excess-baggage charges; I don't give in. Christian is so sweet, calling me his guinea pig, his darling friend, his mummy. And his explanation of Nathalie's[1] birth! She can't be his sister because she didn't come out of my tummy. When he understood, he laughed and seemed quite happy, but I think he's still a bit confused.

Sunday 22 September
It's hard living with friends when you're working, I'm pretty intolerant; this shoot is boring me to death. Luckily, it's Edina, she stays over at my place because she gets scared too. But I'm fine with her, we just eat in front of the TV in t-shirts. We got home pretty late, total relaxation. We try to eat lightly. Stuart seems very happy, but I'm not – his suggestive camerawork annoys me and so does the set. I wish it was over. My parents seem better, I'm happy about that.

Friday 27 September
Final few days, dragging worse than ever. Peter brings me a Hitchcock book, we finish around 6 p.m. but don't get home from shopping until 8.30. Another dinner in front of the TV, laughing, I feel young and lively with Edina.

1 His father Roger Vadim's daughter with Annette Stroyberg.

Saturday 28 September

Last day. Edina and I have been to see Santa Monica. It was like Brittany, the colour and light reminded me of France.

Now that this diary is up to date, I'm going to try not to write just for the sake of it. I'm too suspicious, not considered enough, intellectually lazy. Christian learnt to swim in just eight days, I'm so proud, he trusted me, went underwater with me, the turning point was when he opened his eyes. We took him everywhere – to see dolphins, cowboys – I wasn't always with him, but I was still taking part. I need to be firm and clear with him too. I've got a Paris flight booked for the evening of the 8th. A few days' rest, then I can pack!

Grey skies. Wake up very late. Less than an hour later I'm on my way to do a bit of shopping before I leave this place. Not in a great mood, having so little to do makes me depressed. Feel empty, buy some classical music to cheer myself up. I must make an effort to be more serious and not just concentrate on appearances. I get pleasure from such frivolous things, yet I'm not sixteen anymore. Flaubert said, 'To me, a bourgeois is anyone whose thoughts are base.' Well said. Not to be forgotten.

Light dinner this evening. Watched – for the second time, actually – *The Seven Year Itch*, Marilyn Monroe is dazzling. Then Frankenheimer's *The Train*. I need to take myself back in hand, use this week's freedom well – see new things, read, live, think, stop running around. A telegram came, I know I'm expected in Paris in ten days' time. It's the first time I've been so far away for so long; it's ten weeks now, I hadn't quite realised. At least it's good practice for next time. I'm looking forward to doing *Mississippi Mermaid* even more now, after all these letters from François Truffaut. Though still a little apprehensive.

Sunday 29 September

The day started very late, I slept until noon. Jacques Demy phoned, we're going to have dinner together. It's a little chilly, I don't do much, a bit of mail, the papers, we go to the movies. Delicious dinner with Jacques, chatting. After a few false starts I rediscover the Jacques I know – we have lots in common. We talk about cinema, Godard, Moreau, memories from *The Umbrellas*, a Tristan and Isolde project ... I'm worried that his experience of America has disappointed him, it certainly isn't to my liking, clashes with my sensibilities, it's so dehumanised. Though they do have an interesting way of making fun of themselves, whereas the French are so starchy. All this is shorthand – too lazy to write properly tonight. We also make plans to go to San Francisco on Wednesday, unless Agnès is back.

Monday 30 September

Another short day, I wake at noon. The weather is horrible, overcast. They confirm that shooting will finish on Thursday, I immediately get someone to book me on a Friday flight; it's as good as finished, but then I'm not sure if this film ever really started for me. We'll have to wait and see, I don't want to be too unfair. All the publicity about it must have done me some favours. A bit of shopping this afternoon, found some wonderful classical gramophone records, I even bought the recording of *The Trout* that Marc has. I'll probably spend my last day with Jacques and Agnès. Vadim's got a little girl, Vanessa, which feels very strange – I couldn't really believe it and now here she is.

Tuesday 1 October

More filming. Lunch was a hard-boiled egg in the caravan. I'll be in Paris on Saturday, my heart's bursting. I'll visit Jane Fonda and her new baby on Sunday. I'll sleep late, that'll be nice. If only the weather would cheer up a bit ... What shall I do for Christmas, where will I be? I'm almost twenty-five, I haven't improved myself much: I need to work less, live more.

Thursday 3 October

Waking up was horrible, I had a nightmare. Luckily, the housekeeper Rose came in and interrupted it. The other night, I saw *Gun Crazy* on TV, starring Peggy Cummins and John Dall. Probably the inspiration for *Bonnie and Clyde*, but more violent, more stylish, wonderful dialogue, not at all old-fashioned, makes me think of the temptress character I'm going to play for Truffaut. Heartening letter from my darling mother this morning, I can't wait to see her again. Going over to Jacques's house for dinner tonight, he's sad that I'm leaving so soon. The notion of leaving troubles me a bit, I've hardly seen anyone here, or anything, I haven't done anything, and yet I don't care.

Friday 4 October

So much to do. They've come to take the inventory. It seems you'd really have to fight to salvage anything. My agents arrive to crack open the champagne they gave me. Go to Jacques and Agnès's for dinner. Tom is like Father Christmas with all his presents. Edina puts the big pink satin bow from the champagne bucket on her head.

Time to go, Jacques and Agnès take me to the airport. After such a cheerful dinner, I'm nervous, right in the pit of my stomach. Protected by my big hat. Agnès has tears in her eyes, I want to cry too, Jacques might be enough to bring me back here one day.

Paris. After three hours' flight, the sleeping pill I was given wears off and I wake up, chilled to the bone, and don't get much more sleep. I arrive completely spaced out. Christian is waiting. Don't carry it off too well, I'm tired, I can't sleep, the house is small and cluttered, I'm on edge.

After a difficult wake-up – for me it was dawn, not morning – I get ready quickly. We take Christian out for lunch, and then I can't wait any longer to see Jane's little girl. Same clinic, same room, same birth, same baby, same father. Makes me want to cry. Christian, my big baby, is playing in the courtyard. Jane looks well, sharp and clear-headed as usual. We chat a little about education, although all that is only theory: you don't shape children or impose your ideas on them, you just love them.

Visit my parents, Dad seems to be trying not to show how dejected he is, Mum happy, and more reasonable about my leaving. Not much to say today. I'll go out for lunch with just my dad, and another time with my mother.

The house is tiny, I can't wait to move. If I had the means, no luxury would be too great. But I must trim my expectations.

Monday 7 October
Another visit to my future apartment. Not much needs doing in the immediate term, I'm glad, I'll feel at home very quickly. Lunch with my baby. The massage I'd been needing for ages puts me back on form. Happy to see my agent Giovanella. Go to Saint Laurent's studio again, it's just the same, won't change for years, everything so right, so beautiful.

Sunday 13 October

Alone and weary, I leave Christian with my sister Danièle. Lunch at the Plaza with Hitchcock. He's friendly, open, chatty ... I'm delighted and relaxed, in spite of my swollen cheek from just having had a wisdom tooth removed.

This year promises to be chock-full of projects, but my enthusiasm has run dry.

Wednesday 16 October

Vogue photo shoot before leaving for Switzerland, forget my plane ticket. Watch *Stolen Kisses*: pure, sensitive and moving.

Tuesday 22 October

Leave quickly, rather sad. David is waiting on my doorstep.[1] Met Hakim, the *Mississippi Mermaid* producer, this evening on the plane. Intimate, touching dinner with my parents tonight at my elder sister's place, twenty-five candles on a Saint-Honoré cake for my birthday ... I burst into tears; twenty-five years old, that's how old Françoise was, my sweet beloved sister. She still haunts me at night.

Thursday 24 October

Feel a bit empty. Horribly lacking in concentration and spirit.

This diary was partly written afterwards, from memory. The things that most affected me don't all feature; I didn't dare write everything.

---

1 The author's husband David Bailey.

1991. Posing in Marrakech for André Rau to celebrate the birthday of the wonderful Yves Saint Laurent's design house.

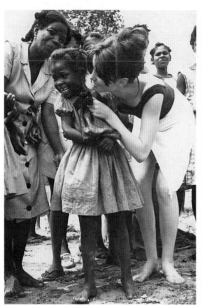

1959. In Cartagena for my first film festival.

2001. La Mamounia Hotel for the Marrakech film festival. With my make-up artist Thibaut. Glass slippers?!

1991. Final week of the *Indochine* shoot, on the banks of a Swiss lake, after three months in Vietnam. Five kilos (eleven pounds) lighter than usual.

Marrakech.
Night-time
observation
during
mating
season.

My first film diary, Los Angeles
1968, written on Japanese paper.

1995. On the set of Raúl Ruiz's *Genealogies of a Crime*. Fantastic set, playing second lead, with Mathieu Amalric.

Cette fois-ci, Solange n'arrive pas à se décider entre le pain et le verre d'eau.

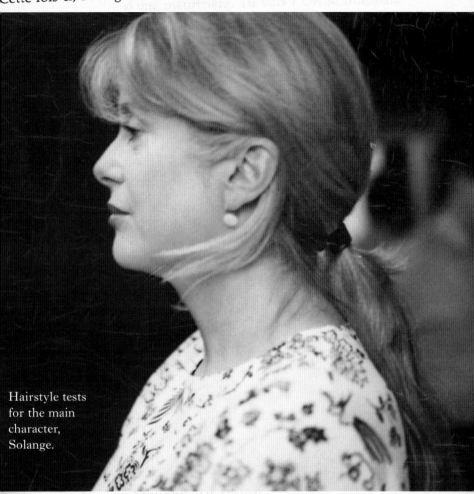

Hairstyle tests
for the main
character,
Solange.

SOLANGE :
Comment va ton analyse ?

LOUISE :
Bien, ça se passe très bien.

SOLANGE :
...Et tu dis que j'ai balancé un chat par la fenêtre.

LOUISE : (ELLE COMMENCE À RIRE)
Un chat dit-elle ! Plusieurs !

SOLANGE :
Ah bon. Ça m'amusait ?

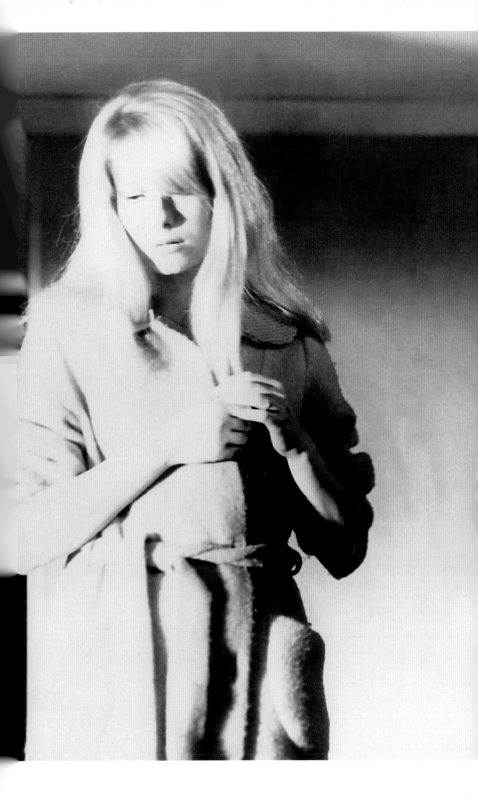

1965. On the set of *Repulsion* with Roman Polanski.

Le Vent de la Nuit

1er jour de tournage 27 Avril - Froid -
vent j'arrive les cheveux mouillé pour faire
la mise en place comme Garel le souhai-
te - Finalement ! - avec de placer la camé-
ra - Tournage chronologique avec du Mark
l'escalier - très beau, 18e très simple -
vert jardin les contremarches - je le sens
heureux en g excité - cheveux longs poivre
et sel - yeux bleus intelligents et rien -
une belle trogne pour cet ancien beau
garçon qui a du bien abusé - En principe
répétitions pour ne tourner qu'une fois si
possible - Il a l'air si sûr de ce qu'il
fait tout en laissant beaucoup de place
à ce qui arrive. Nous tournons en Scope -
" Ne pensez pas à jouer - soyez dans la
pensée - du personnage - soyez simple - les
pensées ça suffit - Si vous pensez vous êtes

My diary about Philippe Garrel's *Night Wind*. Made in 1998.

258   HIGH ANGLE - THE MUSTANG

It moves off down the street.

259   CLOSE SHOT - MOBY DICK

Footage of the whale and Ahab. CAMERA PULLS BACK and ANGLE
WIDENS to reveal Phil in bed watching Moby. He has a high-
ball in his hand and sips the drink as he watches. There is
the SOUND of the front door opening.

>   NICOLE (o.s.)
> Phil... ~~you home?~~ *where are ayou?*
>   PHIL
> In here!

260   NEW ANGLE

He clicks the set off with the remote control. Nicole comes
in. She wears a Masoni pants suit and carries a large Fendi
bag. Her long pale hair cascades loosely but perfectly over
her shoulders. She drops the bag, looks at him, and slowly
unbuttons her blouse.

>   PHIL
> Listen, about the other night --
> goddammit I... I want you to know
> I never see any sins with you.
> ~~All my sins are in the mirror.~~

Her blouse is off, she unstraps her bra. She says nothing.

261   CLOSE ON PHIL

> We had a d[...]
> ~~I do mine..~~
> what you do[...]
> ~~do,~~ and it [...]
> ~~crazy about~~ *I love ye[...]*
> been. I sm[...] *I knew but*
> all day. Y[...] *didn't think*
> I'm saying, *you would*
> out -- we'll *never say it*
> ~~we'll be tho~~[...]

Her head and naked bac[...] top of him. She kisses[...]

1968. Robert Aldrich and
Burt Reynolds sent me the
provisional script for *The April
Fools* with my name engraved
on the front, in an effort to
recruit m[...]

All The Other Angels

CATHERINE DENEUVE AS *"Nicole"*

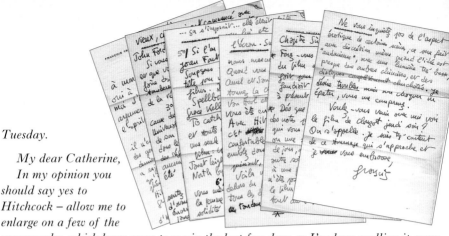

Tuesday.

My dear Catherine,
In my opinion you
should say yes to
Hitchcock – allow me to
enlarge on a few of the
reasons why, which have come to me in the last few days as I've been mulling it over:

1. *Hitchcock isn't too old, or 'finished'. If you speak to people who've been around Buñuel recently, they'll all tell you that he's ten years younger than he was three years ago.*

2. *At the moment, the best directors in Hollywood are the oldest ones, those that started out making silent films: John Ford, Hawks, Cukor and Hitch. If you don't work with them but still want to make films in English, you're bound to end up with TV renegades, nearly all shirkers.*

3. *Because of his contract with Universal, and the worldwide regard for his work, a Hitchcock film is heavily promoted throughout the whole world, and penetrates into places where I doubt your previous films have ever been screened.*

4. *Hitchcock-Deneuve! You must be able to see that this partnership would make anticipation of the film absolutely immense. Everyone who hadn't yet thought of it will exclaim 'but of course… it was meant to be… she was made for him, etc…*

5. *If someone mentioned Joan Fontaine, you'd think of* Rebecca *and* Suspicion, *and probably couldn't bring to mind any other films she's done; Ingrid Bergman:* Notorious, Spellbound; *Grace Kelly:* Dial M for Murder, To Catch a Thief, Rear Window… *then there's all the actresses he's only worked with once, but in each case that's her best film: Kim Novak -* Vertigo, *Janet Leigh -* Psycho, *Eva Marie Saint -* North by Northwest, *etc…*

6. *You've felt yourself how pleasant it is to be a woman flanked by two men, and this dynamic helps to create a solid basis on screen. Especially if you're playing with two big male names - when you made* Manon *you were helping Jean Aurel and Sami Frey, when you made* Heartbeat *you were helping Cavalier, Von Hool and Piccolli, and inevitably, this meant that each time, you were endangering yourself. With Hitch and two big co-stars it's different, you're comfortable from the outset, you're flying in a safe, proven, powerful and reassuring aeroplane.*

So that's my point of view, quite apart from the fact that I love you both, and imagining you 'in tandem' gives me a lot of pleasure.
About Mississippi Mermaid:

Are you happy to do the English dubbing of the film afterwards? Have you done that for your recent films? We need to get this clear now. As soon as you receive the script, take notes so that you can show me which scenes make you anxious, for whatever reason. We'll avoid the unfortunate problems of the Belle de Jour *shoot which you described to me the other evening by being totally frank with each other; if you're not happy on this shoot, the film will suffer - more than any other film.*

Don't worry about the erotic side to some of the scenes: it will be shot very discreetly even at the moments where the idea is 'daring' - very low lighting, almost a shadow show, and the dialogue all whispered. I want to arouse the audience, but not shock them, you know what I mean.

Would you like to see the Clouzot film with me on Thursday evening?

Let's call each other. I'm so happy about making this movie, and I send you a big kiss,

François.

Catherine, dear Catherine,

> *The camera*
> *The audience*
> *Your directors*
> *Your co-stars*
> *Movie-buffs around the world…*
> *All love you*
>
> *And me, and me, and me…*

So don't let yourself slide; the show must go on and you too, because you're part of the show.

I'm sending you the biggest kiss ever,

François.

Right: 1980. For *The Last Metro.* François says: Hello, and then it'll be: action, and then: cut. With love, F.

Left: Truffaut gave me this note on my first day on the *Once Upon a Time* set, in 1970.

LES FILMS DU CARROSSE

5, RUE ROBERT ESTIENNE, PARIS-8   TÉL. 256-12-73

The cigarette packet for *Mississippi Mermaid.*

Children in Hué.

1991. In Vietnam, during the filming of *Indochine*.

With Régis Wargnier.

The Imperial City of Hué.

A film, an adventure, a journey. I was completely bowled over by Vietnam.

Hotel jewellery box. Thieving magpie!

Chère madame,   13 2 96

Voici le roman (1850). Si vous ne l'aimiez pas, ou le personnage de la mère, je pourrais toujours vous convaincre que mon film en est éloigné. Si vous l'aimiez trop, je serais plus embarassé pour vous faire lire mon projet.

Je veux faire ce film avec vous.

J'ai aimé vous voir. Comme le suggère le court rêve que je vous ai passé (sans grand intéret, sauf pour moi), il existe "un lien" entre nous. Si nous avons l'occasion de nous connaitre un jour, je vous raconterai.

Portez vous belle et bien

[handwritten margin notes, partly illegible]

Je suis inquiet :
...-j...able ...
... de signer ...
Avez vous des nouvelles

13 2 96

Dear Madam,

Here is the novel (1850). If you don't like it, or the character of the mother, I can always persuade you that my film is a loose adaptation. If you like it too much, I'll be even more nervous about having you read the screenplay.

I want to make this film with you.

I liked seeing you. As the short dream I had about you suggests (not of great interest in itself, apart from for me), there is 'a bond' between us. If we have the opportunity to get to know each other one day, I'll tell you the dream.

Take good care of yourself,

Love,
LC.

I'm worried: Guillaume D. isn't well… unbelievable… but apparently about to sign another film contract. Do you have any news?

LARS VON TRIER   22/8 - 95

DEAR CATHRINE
THANK YOU FOR YOUR LETTER!
I SEE YOU EVERY DAY (AND YOU
DON'T SEE ME) BUT YOU ARE COOKING
SO GOOD! I CAN'T WAIT TO
SHOW YOU SOMETHING…
WHO KNOWS, BY THE END

Interview
with Pascal Bonitzer
2004

We might as well start by calling a spade a spade . . .

And Catherine a little minx . . .

And Catherine a star. There's something a little bewildering about these logbooks, or work journals, because people don't tend to think of film stars as working.

Well, I'm not sure that people think 'film star'. They think of my image, my portrayals, Cannes . . . and anyway, I don't think of it that way myself, because it isn't really work, more like a constant preoccupation. For me, real work would be performing on stage, learning your words by heart, rehearsing with the other actors, having to start the same thing from scratch each day. Film shoots are much more subtle than that; it's quite unique. Of course, there are some constraints – getting up early, shooting at weird hours – so you could call it a job. But I don't think people want to know about that, because with actors who they see on the screen, like me . . . in the end, it's like going to the opera: you see a ballet, you like it or you hate it but it's something finite, complete in itself, you don't see the dancers suffering as they rehearse.

What I mean is that these diaries portray an unknown side of you, the working actress rather than the movie star.

Yes, of course, that's true, and especially because I don't find it easy to talk about that side. In fact, I refuse to. I don't talk much in general. During interviews journalists hardly ever question you on the making of the film. Just lots of rapid-fire questions and then a discussion of your next film. And because they aren't really asking or wanting to know, I don't take it any further than they do. These diaries are a thing apart. To start with, they're very disjointed, in that I wrote some of them a long time ago, and, apart from one, all on foreign shoots, on films where I wasn't overly busy, or surrounded by too many people. I wrote them mostly in the evenings, unless we had to film early the next morning, or during lunch breaks.

And what made you want to start writing? The first of these diaries was written in 1968 . . .

I have to say it began with a lonely, rather difficult time. Going to film abroad, so far from home, and knowing I was so eagerly awaited, because according to the papers, the Americans saw me as the most beautiful actress around . . . I tried not to think about it, but it was a lot of pressure.

You were already having to live up to the 'French movie star' label . . .

Not so much star as beauty. Which is even more pressure. It warps the connection from the outset, if you see what I mean. It's not that the challenge is too high, but that it's just at the *wrong* height, because you've already had to leave your city, your life, your friends . . . I was rather afraid of spending three months filming in the United States. I remember my agent at the time, an Italian woman by the name of Giovanella Giannoni, telling me that things were going to be very tough. It was after May

'68. I think she really believed what she was saying, but she also thought that I needed to be pushed to leave, because she knew how much – maybe too much – I treasured my family life and my baby son. It was a hard time on a personal level; I'd lost my sister the previous year. I hadn't ... got over it. Actually, that's not quite the right word. I wasn't really all there. Going away wasn't a solution, but I think she knew that I needed a push, and it really was a troubled time, the future of French cinema did look very bleak. So she told me, 'I don't know where European cinema is going, and it's a very good proposition, in my opinion you should consider it seriously,' because she knew how reluctant I was to go to the States for three months.

It really was such an intense time in your personal life. The repercussions of your sister's tragic demise ...

Yes, Françoise ...

... and at such a turbulent time for cinema, and the world in general.

Yes, and I was also feeling that I had a lot of things to take care of: I was single, I had my son, a lot of responsibilities. It was a good decision for me, and from a certain perspective, very sensible.

There's an almost therapeutic feel to that first diary, some kind of imperative to write things down straight away, and maybe also a sort of intention-setting, evident for example when you write: 'I must make an effort to be more serious, and not just concentrate on appearances.'

They were absolutely determined that I do the film ... I could sense that what I represented for them was not quite how I saw myself. But at the same time, you have to live up to what people are expecting. Having to be that person, physically, takes effort – it doesn't come naturally. And sometimes it's a distraction from the work, if I can put it like that. So on this film shoot I was trying to rediscover my focus. But I could feel myself getting lost anyway ... well, getting lost ... let's just say I would tend to lose myself in carefree oblivion, as a way of dealing with that challenge. I'm pretty manic-depressive. I have moments of unconcern, followed by moments of sadness, and on it goes ...

But did this perhaps mark a new phase in your life, a striving for maturity?

Well yes, it did. Both out of duty and because that's the situation I found myself in. I was more alone than usual, and at the same time, highly aware of what the future was likely to bring. I was working a lot, and I'd already worked hard during '67 and '68 – I'd shot two films back to back. Which, in the state I was in ... But it took me a very, very long time to reach maturity. I'm not even sure I've reached it now ...

These logbooks describe some people you were very keen to work with, but not really the filmmakers to whom you have been closest – I'm thinking of Truffaut and Téchiné.

That's true, perhaps I also kept the diaries to offset a lack of something ... they were often written when I felt a bit lonely, with regard to the film I was shooting.

Furthermore your diaries are very discreet about your private life. You're a rather discreet person in general.

Yes, because I've got respect for ... well ... to tell you the truth, it seems to me that the diaries were always written as a compensation for either a kind of sadness, or a lack of something, an emotional lack ...

Not always. For example the longest diary ...

About *Indochine?*

Yes, the Indochine *diary, on the contrary, was a result of the length of the shoot.*

Well yes, absolutely, but with *Indochine* I was also very far away, and really very cut off from my world. It was incredibly exotic, especially as I went for a long time, with long periods when I wasn't shooting. I had time, time to see the country, time to see people ... the film really blew me away ... and then it also had to do with Régis Wargnier's personality; we did the film together, we found each other on that film. You see, Régis has quite an inflexible side to him ...

'Military background' ...

Yes, exactly. When you say you'll do something, you do it, when you say you're going to do a screening, you do one. It was simultaneously rigid and comforting. Because while structure can sometimes be annoying, with such a huge shoot and so many people, it's also reassuring.

Yet with Tristana, *for instance, you can hardly say it was a very long way from home: it was shot in Madrid* ...

But it was abroad. In Toledo, and then in the Madrid studio.

It was the second time you had worked with Buñuel ...

It felt very important to me to work with him again after *Belle de Jour*, which wasn't a terribly positive experience. I was hugely impressed with the *Tristana* script, but apprehensive, because I kept remembering the difficult times I'd had shooting *Belle de Jour*. Buñuel had been surrounded by protective producers, and we didn't talk much. It was different with *Tristana* because we shot in Spain. And it was the first time he'd worked in Spain since *Viridiana*. All that was very important for him, whereas I was going through a rough time in my personal life. I was quite fragile. It really wasn't that easy.

You say that the Belle de Jour *shoot wasn't a good experience. The subject matter was extremely intense, and you were very exposed* ...

Very exposed in every sense of the word, but very exposed physically, which caused me distress; I felt they showed more of me than they'd said they were going to. I saw it again recently, in a great new print in the United States. I think it's a wonderful film, but ... the producers isolated Buñuel, I couldn't really talk to him, or see the rushes. There were moments when I felt totally used. I was very unhappy. And my sister was crucial at that time, she gave me a lot of moral support during the shoot, she was really there for me, very strong. It was only afterwards that I realised how much Françoise . . . you know, it's hard to talk about the challenges of being an actress, unless you have a close actress friend, which I don't, and I realised how much I was missing Françoise, how much I missed being able to share in the way you only can when you're personally close and do the same kind of work . . . these days, I sometimes get that with my daughter. Because we have a very close relationship and she's an actress too.

So, although it hadn't been an easy experience, you chose to work with him again. And what about Buñuel, how did he . . .?

I don't think he had the same recollection of *Belle de Jour*, otherwise he wouldn't have asked me to play Tristana. But at the same time, he has quite a simplistic view of actors . . . I imagine he thought that seeing as I was right for the character, he'd better give me the role. End of story. I think he thought that while actors were important, they weren't the main thing. In any case, he didn't talk to his actors much.

It's even said that while he was certainly a bit deaf, he sometimes used to exaggerate the problem.

I don't think he exaggerated. He wasn't exactly deaf, but he really couldn't hear very well. I think he also used to turn down his hearing aid when it was getting on his nerves, or when it suited him to do so. It's extremely tiring giving directions on set and paying close attention to everything.

That's true. The Tristana *shoot clearly wasn't a bundle of laughs either . . .*

No, it wasn't! But in the end, you know, it was actually rather a wonderful shoot. And one tends to confide in a diary at the hardest times ...

It's one of your best roles.

Yes, *Tristana* is one of my favourite films. Personally, as an actress, I prefer *Tristana* to *Belle de Jour*.

They're like two aspects of ... that is, they're almost opposites, like de Sade's Juliette *and* Justine.

Yes, that's true.

Because Tristana *is a cruel film ... a film about becoming old, about a man's senescence ...*

Oh yes, it's a very dark film.

So the diary was a kind of support for that as well?

Yes, support, and also, at a certain stage, the desire to put things in writing ... there are so many things you don't remember later. I've got a lot of respect for people who keep a daily diary. And diaries are powerful too: when you find them again, read them again, it's amazing what they bring back – images, memories, surfacing with a degree of clarity that the person who wrote the diary might never have expected.

What's special about yours is the rate at which it's written ... professional diarists organise their time around writing, they choose exactly the right moment. Whereas with yours the urgency is palpable.

I think that's also because I was often writing late at night, after the day's shoot . . .

Did it take a lot of discipline? Was it a matter of forcing yourself to write?

You know, the trouble was time. One finishes late, and I always need some time to unwind, I really have to make a clean break after a shoot; then it's bedtime, and when I'm working I try to go to sleep as soon as I'm in bed. But in the end, that's also how I am; I often work in a hurry, unfortunately . . . but that's just the way it is. There really isn't much time after filming. Especially when you're shooting abroad, the film seems to take over your life much more than when you're in Paris and can go home to your life, your children, your friends . . .

That's also a consequence of living in hotels, on your own . . .

Yes. I've never kept a diary in Paris. André Téchiné and I filmed in the French countryside, but not abroad, and it's not the same. You're not cut off from the world in the same way. Besides, it's often not carefully written, it's an on-the-spot diary. Diaries are supposed to be private . . . though that depends. Some people do write diaries with the intention of publishing them . . . mine is more of a logbook, which didn't stop me from censoring myself, because I'm quite judgemental, and I know that there are things I refrained from saying, even in my notes. Even when something seems harmless to you, it can be interpreted as cruelty, and what's the point of that? It's not about watering things down, just that the power of the written word can be terrible, terrible . . .

Cruel.

And also, which is what frightens me, the written word is really cast in stone. You can have regrets, you can deny it, say it was printed without your agreement, that your words were changed ... none of that alters the fact that what's written is written. The printed word has the weight of absolute truth. And this weight of truth endures longer than one could ever imagine.

When you were keeping these notes, you weren't thinking about ...

Oh no, not at all. No, never!

But you still had the concern that ...

That it might be read? I didn't think about it. But then, what's strange is that I kept them. OK, I haven't moved house much in my life, but still, they've always been close to me, in a desk in my bedroom, not that I've ever been tempted to re-read them.

You didn't write for years and years ...

No. Wait a minute, what year was *Tristana*? 1969?

Yes, Tristana *was 1969. And then nothing until ...*

The thing is, after that I did go into a decline, you know.

Into a decline?

Yes. On a personal level, I went into a decline, yes.

Do you mean after 1970?

What year was Chiara born? She's almost thirty-two, so she was born ... when? In 1972. Yes, that period was a total black-out for me. Anyway, what films did I do during that time? That would be interesting ... I must still have been filming, even in that state ... I must have filmed ... when did I do *Once Upon a Time?*

Once Upon a Time *must have been 1970.*

Yes, it must've been around that time. I was really out of it.

It was the first film you made with Jacques Demy since The Young Girls of Rochefort.

Yes, but I almost couldn't do the film. I was in such bad physical health that I could hardly do anything, never mind write. What's the next logbook?

Indochine, *1991.*

In any case, the fact is I didn't write during that whole time because I couldn't, or because I didn't need or want to. That period was a fight for life! A real matter of life and death. The fight. A fight. A fight that took all my energy.

You're sure you didn't write anything between 1969 and 1991?

I don't think so. I must have spent less time on my own

during those shoots. And it was also then that I had my daughter.

So during that the time you were being a mother ... And therefore there's nothing until 1991, Indochine, more than twenty years later.

Yes, I came back to it when I had the space, the desire, the curiosity ...

And the tone at this point is completely different, more excited and elated.

Because it wasn't just a film, it was an adventure, a huge journey ... great role, great subject, great country, those tiny individuals making up a great people, I was hugely impressed by the Vietnamese. Hugely.

And you hadn't anticipated this at all?

I hadn't thought it would fascinate me to that extent. The people's tenacity and calm were unbelievable, somehow eternal and yet, at the same time, incredibly active, deeply energetic but not at all restless. Yes, Asia is very special.

So you had a deep connection with Régis?

A deep connection, yes. It was a subject he had chosen for me. I met him when he was assisting Francis Girod on *Le Bon Plaisir*. He hadn't made a film at that stage, we talked about it, I said to him well yes, why not, if he wanted to write a film for me. He wrote the plot thinking of me, and it's true that it was a very thrilling adventure. A big project, a big film, it was all in there ...

And a long diary.

And a long diary! Well, long . . .

Long compared with the others. Of course, that also had to do with the length of the shoot.

Yes, but not only. Not only. It was also twenty years later.

Had you met Vincent Perez before starting Indochine?

We all met each other very formally before the shoot, you know, in the office . . .

Did you do a read-through of the screenplay?

No, Régis works a bit like Truffaut. It's him that holds the readings. That's my favourite way of rehearsing, reading with only the director present. Later, you might want to all read together, but when several of you read, you don't get that intimacy, and you can't linger over certain scenes, you just have a quick run-through and off you go. It must be different in the theatre, but to me, in the movies, read-throughs aren't much use. So I think I did a reading with just Régis and Vincent. He had a difficult role, Régis was watching him very closely, more so than me . . .

In any case you give the impression that it was a happy shoot, despite the accidents and the storms . . .

Yes, it really was wonderful, more than a film shoot, an adventure. Also four months' filming is a long time, a whole period, it knocks your life sideways.

135

And then a diary for East–West; *was that because being in Sofia, Bulgaria, was another kind of exoticism?*

It was also because I had time, and what's more, I was probably nostalgic for *Indochine*. But I struggled to really enter into that film because I wasn't at the heart of it, even if Régis had written the role especially for me. I was always saying that actors don't often take supporting roles, although I think some second roles are fantastic, and he said, 'What if I wrote you a big supporting role?' I said sure, why not? He challenged me to take it, and as it was a lovely part, I did. Some supporting roles are boring – for me, the criteria must be whether the film would remain the same without that character. If it would, the supporting role isn't a good one.

It doesn't often happen in French cinema that a star takes a supporting role . . .

Because often supporting roles are written without any proper scenes for the actor to get their teeth into. I wanted it to be a wonderful, real role, even if it was short. I also took a supporting role in *Tom Thumb*, and then *A Talking Picture* by Manoel de Oliveira. Though it was a bit different with Oliveira, that was a reunion.

Some directors you just wanted to work with because of who they are.

Yes.

For instance, your part in Lars von Trier's Dancer in the Dark *is also a supporting role; you took it because you were curious about the filmmaker . . .*

Yes, absolutely, because I didn't find the role exactly riveting, frankly.

It isn't.

No. It was the process, the adventure of making the film that I was interested in.

Björk clearly took centre stage.

She was absolutely at the heart of the film; it was a very hard and a very heavy role. She did suffer, but she used to protect herself a lot, surrounding herself with her gang. She was never alone. And also she wasn't staying at the hotel; she'd rented a house and brought some friends over, her sound engineer, her son, her son's friends, she'd had a studio installed so that she could work. She'd re-created her Icelandic universe.

You go through a whole spectrum of feelings about her. And you're not the only one . . .

There were times when I really wanted to . . . I lost heart towards the end. You feel loyal to the director, and yet at the same time, you get angry, you want to say, 'Listen, you sort yourselves out, I'll be in Paris, you can call when you need me, I'm getting out of here too.' I could have . . .

Yes.

But basically I'm a good girl. I just complain, like a proper Frenchwoman, bitch and complain.

Night Wind *is the exception that confirms the rule, in that it wasn't shot overseas. So what was the exotic aspect of that film?*

I think because it was so experimental. Because it was Garrel, and Garrel is unique. For instance, he decided to shoot the film exclusively in single takes, with the exception of technical hiccups.

I think he has a theory about that: he says that actors are like batteries; they start to run down as soon as filming begins.

It's funny that he should say that, because I'm always saying that I sleep a lot during film shoots. When people ask me, 'What do you get up to on shoots while you're waiting?' I reply, 'I sleep, I recharge myself.' You see, I'm the perfect Garrel actress! He comes across as very confident about what he's doing, while leaving a lot of space for spontaneity. He used to say to me, 'Don't think about acting. Just be in the character's thoughts, be simple. Her thoughts are enough. If you're thinking right, you'll be right.' It sounds very simple, but in order to tell your actors something so simple, you really have to have thought things through. 'If you think right, you'll be right.'

Being in the character's thoughts is hardly easy.

Being in the character's thoughts, no, it isn't, because it means being able to disregard everything around you: the crew, the technical constraints. It's hard to actually feel like you're someone else when that person is very different from you. Normally, you act by drawing on your own experience.

Was the script completely written?

Yes, it was a wonderful screenplay. The film was born of a desire to work together. He lives in the same neighbourhood, you see; we were always bumping into each other, he'd said that he would love to make a film with me, and I'd said likewise. I love his films, I find them very moving – poetic, crazy, full of love and extremely personal. So he said, 'OK, why not?', and went off to write something, actually no, not just anything, he wanted to build something around me. I told him that was exactly what I didn't want. I like to act, not to play myself ... well not too closely, anyway. He was a bit disappointed, and then he did some collaboration with Marc Cholodenko. They wrote the screenplay, which I thought was fantastic. I really, really love the story ... I very much enjoyed making *Night Wind*. It's very simple, and yet extremely compelling about what links people together, what makes you accept people even when they're different from you ... it's a very powerful, yet somehow pure film.

Have you seen the films he made in the 1970s, the really experimental ones?

No, not really. I think I've seen one. One of my favourites is *I Don't Hear the Guitar Anymore* ...

That's from his second period.

Yes, I've hardly seen anything from his first period. At

that time, I was hearing a lot about him, rather than actually seeing his films.

Caroline Champetier was already the camerawoman in I Don't Hear the Guitar Anymore, *wasn't she? What about* Night Wind?

That was Caroline too.

You've ended up doing quite a few films with her, and also working with her on both your TV series, Josée Dayan's Les Liaisons dangereuses *and Benoît Jacquot's* Marie Bonaparte.

Yes. She's complicated, because she's such a bright and passionate woman. The problem is that sometimes she tries to take over more than just the camerawork, and I don't know if she even knows she's doing it. On the other hand, you rarely see a cameraman or woman getting so involved in the film, never losing her concentration, never, never. She's on set the whole time, and not just passively; she's there because she's always on to everything: the direction, the actors . . . she takes a great interest in the actors and her viewpoints are fascinating. She's demanding, the constancy and intensity of her presence on a shoot is totally unique. She and Garrel were sometimes in conflict. They know each other well, admire each other, love each other deeply, but Philippe would sometimes be a bit ferocious with her. It was the only way of keeping her in her place. Some directors wouldn't be able to handle working with someone as forceful as her.

You've covered almost the whole range of cinema . . . from big

commercial projects to radical writer-directors like Ferreri,
Ruiz, Oliveira, Carax, Garrel.

No, there are some directors I've never worked with, like
Sautet for instance. In fact, I was going to work with him,
but it never happened – there were problems with agents
and producers. And Régis and I almost went down that
route – I didn't want to do his first film although I'd told
him, when he was an assistant director, that I would.

The one he did with Jane Birkin?

Yes, but I don't really like talking about films that I've
passed up. It doesn't seem very respectful to the people
who did make them. I was due to do a film with Régis, I
didn't want to do that one, so be it, tough luck, but that
didn't stop him from wanting to approach me again a few
years later. Although I do understand that being said 'no'
to can feel like a rejection.

Maybe there are two kinds of man . . .

Some who won't take 'no' for an answer?

Exactly.

Not definitively in any case.

Lots of women don't understand 'no' either.

Yes, I must say I'm often stubborn and obstinate and
won't take 'no' for an answer myself.

Are there any filmmakers you would have liked to work with but who haven't wanted to work with you?

Not so much who didn't want to work with me, but where initial negotiations came to nothing. There's one director I would have loved to work with, well actually, it was a particular film I really wanted to do ... what's his name ...? I thought the screenplay was fantastic, I met him in Paris, he's a big producer now, and also an actor for Woody Allen and Stanley Kubrick.

Sydney Pollack?

Sydney Pollack. Marthe Keller got the role in the end. It's a love story between her – she's very ill – and a racing-car driver played by Al Pacino. And there's another film from around the same time that I really wanted to do, it's such a wonderful subject – *The Bridges of Madison County*. They looked at dozens of European actresses, I even went to London for an audition, and then they chose Meryl Streep. In the novel the woman is a European living in the States, but hey ... in the end, Clint Eastwood starred and directed.

How did you meet Leos Carax?

I'd enjoyed his film *Bad Blood*. And then he came to me with an unusual request: he was struggling to get *Pola X* made and wanted me to film a few shots, so that he could make a fifteen-minute clip to take to Cannes with a view to raising finance. I'd read the screenplay and had a few reservations, especially about the length. So I said to him, 'OK, but I'm not promising that I'll make the film itself.'

Though in the end, I did, because my wish to work with Carax was stronger than my doubts.

That too was quite an experience.

Yes, though the shoot itself went better than the release of the film. When I saw it, the flaws I'd noticed in the screenplay were still there. My role wasn't a large one, and as it had been heavily cut, and I had a lot of reservations about the film, I didn't want to go to the Cannes press conference, where the film was presented, and he was rather crass about that ... I never thought it was a good idea to show it at Cannes, but I still went to the première because not going would have been like a very public slap in the face. I didn't go to the press conference because I didn't want to put myself in the position of having to respond to journalists' questions. I had too many reservations. And I think he took that badly, so when someone asked why I wasn't there, he gave a nasty reply. I think he said I was at the hairdresser! When I saw him, I said, 'Frankly, that was neither honest nor gallant of you, given that I'm showing my support of your film by my presence tonight.' He was very apologetic, he'd got carried away, and I think he was quite upset ... and then the film got the reception it got. When you've made a film, you have to take responsibility for it, unfortunately. I say 'unfortunately' because, once you achieve a certain level of notoriety, you have to own whatever you've done, even if you don't feel comfortable with the final product ... and in Carax's film ... I only featured in about a third of it. So when I saw it on the screen, it looked very different. When you cut scenes in that way, and with an actress who only features in part of the film ... I really think he should have warned me before the screening.

And I did find the film a little disappointing. To be honest, the second half wasn't . . .

The screenplay . . .

Carax would do well to work with a scriptwriter, but there aren't enough scriptwriters anymore, because unfortunately, they all become directors, well unfortunately for us, the actors. In my opinion French copyright laws are excessive, they don't always serve the director, they isolate him or her. I think you can be a writer-director and yet be willing to share, discuss, criticise and change things. French copyright gives the omniscient *auteur* inordinate rights while taking away those of the producer. This really isolates the director and puts inhuman amounts of pressure on them to excel.

Speaking of omniscient auteurs, *what was your experience of working with Raúl Ruiz?*

I loved it. I trusted him implicitly, as soon as I met him I knew he was a real filmmaker, an intelligent, cultured man who would be a pleasure to work with; I could tell he would be resourceful and courteous. Raúl gives his actors a lot of freedom, whereas Manoel de Oliveira is extremely controlling when he directs, and quite radical – we shot *The Convent* with no dolly or zoom lens. So at certain points, you had to turn right around and speak to the camera, things like that were rather . . . let's just say that for an actor it was an interesting stylistic experiment, but definitely much more hard-core.

More rigid.

Yes, more rigid. Manoel has a great sense of humour, he's mischievous and rigid at the same time. Not like Raúl. Raúl lets things flow with the actors, he watches them and uses what he likes . . .

And he's very resourceful with his camerawork.

Yes. And when you're rehearsing, he's extremely open to whatever comes up. Whereas Manoel knows exactly what he's trying to do, and also these days is constantly reworking things on his computer, it's very intense; he always has done a lot of reworking, but now he does it in the evenings, constantly . . . rewriting, no less, and then turning up in the morning with all this new stuff he's typed out, altering dialogues and giving the actors new directions.

Manoel?

Yes, yes, Manoel. Once the shoot is finished for the day. And they generally don't finish late because he starts very early in the morning. What's more, he drinks a lot of coffee and eats very little. He's a sharp man for his age, the oldest filmmaker around, and one of the best . . .

. . . in the world . . .

In the world. And in spirit one of the youngest, well not quite the youngest, but he's very young in spirit, really, with an unbelievable amount of energy. But now he's started reworking stuff in the evenings, which is a nightmare for everyone involved. In any case, I think he hardly sleeps.

You've also done two films with another radical filmmaker, Ferreri.

Yes, but I wouldn't have done three. It wasn't what I'd call a deep encounter. Like everyone else's, my part in *Don't Touch the White Woman!* was a cameo rather than a real role, which wasn't the case for *Love to Eternity*. I found Ferreri's personality . . .

. . . a hindrance?

Something like that. I might admire someone, or find it interesting to work with them, but there's got to be something beyond the film if we're going to stay in touch; I've got to like the person. When you do a second film with someone, a relationship starts to form. I couldn't imagine doing five films with a director I only knew on set, with whom I didn't have any other kind of warm or intimate connection.

Do most actors have this experience of him?

No. For me the problem was his relationship to life. He made people uneasy. I found him quite unsettling, maybe because he struggled with the fact that his most successful films weren't his greatest or most ambitious. I sensed a kind of violence in him, not the verbal violence of shy, neurotic people who have to shout to get any respect . . . it was something else. To start with I found it terrifying, but then it became helpful; I became tougher once I realised his ferocity didn't impress me.

But he wasn't a bad man?

Well, he wasn't exactly a nice man. Our last meetings were very raw, he was extremely aggressive, almost violent towards me.

After Don't Touch the White Woman!*?*

Yes, a while after, when Marcello died[1]. They were close friends, they spent time together, and while I was living with him, we spent time together too. You know what Italians are like: they live in each other's pockets.

So it was completely the opposite to André Téchiné?

Oh yes! André is very reserved, we got on well immediately, but proper friendships take a long time to develop. We were drawn to see each other outside of film shoots, he doesn't see many people and actually neither do I. We went to the movies together, I even went on holiday with him! Friendship is important to me. Extremely important. Besides, all my real friends have been friends for a long time.

Téchiné is the director with whom you've done the most films. He and Gilles Taurand wrote Hotel America *with you in mind . . .*

André often works like that. *Scene of the Crime, My Favourite Season, Thieves . . .*

Yes, he's a filmmaker who writes with actors already in mind. Did you know him at all when you were sent the

---

[1] Marcello Mastroianni, with whom the author had a daughter, Chiara.

screenplay for Hotel America? *Had you seen any of his films?*

No, I didn't know him at all. Our mutual agent Gérard Lebovici arranged the meeting, because André was even more shy then than he is today.

And you didn't feel the need to keep a diary on that film, even though it was shot abroad ...?

I didn't keep a diary on any of André's shoots. His films take up the whole time and space, and also I don't think I was alone in the evenings on those films, and it's usually in the evenings that I write. When I'm filming with André I spend a lot of time with him.

Right from the first film?

Yes, I seem to remember that we saw each other a lot. But it's funny because on the second film, no, not the second, when we did *My Favourite Season*, we sometimes used to spend the evening with Daniel Auteuil as well. The idea was that we'd talk about the film, the issues coming up, but in the end, we never talked about the film. Though strangely enough, we did talk about it in a very indirect way. We'd always return to the film without ever directly saying 'OK, so this week, there's this scene to shoot', or broaching particular questions that we had. We did have questions, but somehow, when we ate together in the evening, we ate together as friends. Which was very nice, and quite unusual.

Had you already done a film with Daniel Auteuil?

No. That was the first. Now that *was* a deep encounter. He's really someone I'm very fond of ... usually, men and women play husbands and wives, or lovers and mistresses, whereas the fact of playing a brother and sister meant that we formed a kind of intimate, fraternal friendship. In fact, that first on-set meeting defined the nature of our relationship. At our age it's very rare to play a brother and sister, and meeting as brother and sister in a film for the first time aged forty-five ... we speak on the phone and meet up from time to time. Sometimes with Vincent Lindon.

In contrast, the actor Patrick Dewaere, your co-star in Hotel America, *comes from a totally different universe ...*

He was very touching, but he came from such a far away world that it was hard to get close to him.

Which is part of what the film's about, anyway.

Both the film and the shoot. I hardly ever had dinner just with him. His wife was there as well, she'd come to be with him, and they were going through a very complicated, painful time, which didn't make it easy for us to be friends. But I did find his particular blend of bewilderment and despair – no, not despair, disappointment – rather moving. It was a difficult time for him because he'd come completely off drugs so he'd be clean before filming began.

He committed suicide not long after?

He killed himself before doing Lelouch's film about

Marcel Cerdan. He came home from one of their rehearsals and . . .

Your co-star in Scene of the Crime *was Wadeck Stanczack.*

I think he looks like Jesus. André always chooses me nice lovers and admirers, but I'm not so sure about the partners and husbands. One day, I said to him, 'You'd better let me read the script first next time!' He always wants to give me corpulent, fleshy partners, people one could imagine I might have married in a fit of youthful enthusiasm.

In any case, the women you play in his films always have a horrible time with their husbands . . . In Scene of the Crime, *if I remember rightly, you're virtually raped by Victor Lanoux, and in* My Favourite Season *you leave your husband after telling him some home truths that are . . .*

Sad, and very hard to hear.

Your daughter, Chiara, also had her first role in My Favourite Season.

Yes, that's right. Everyone asks me about that, but you know, I hardly filmed anything with her apart from that Christmas dinner scene. She knew I was nearby, but we weren't shooting together.

Did she already want to be an actress at that time?

It was very hard for me to know. I think she had, for a long time, but she hadn't told me. She used to talk about writing, rather . . .

It takes guts to go into acting when your parents are Mastroianni and Deneuve ...

You're a bit oblivious when you're young. At the beginning, she didn't realise quite what she was doing – I think it may have become more difficult later. Luckily, she did her first film with André, which is wonderful.

He's like family.

Yes. And also Chiara knew his films, she's a real film buff, very well informed.

And André works very closely with his actors.

Very closely. He even whispers to them, like Truffaut.

Another thing about Truffaut was his persistence ...

They're both people who really know what they want. It's fine for directors to not know quite how to achieve a certain effect, but they've got to know what they want or what they're looking for. And some won't give up until they've got it. Not everyone can do that, it's a luxury you're not always given. Truffaut and Téchiné used to make sure they had enough time to rehearse, and to rework things, whereas today you first and foremost have to film quickly. Too many directors give in to this frenetic pace, usually imposed by the technical department.

In your Dancer in the Dark *notes, you allude to a horrible scene with André on the set of* Thieves ...

We had an argument that really traumatised me. But it's interesting, because it hit me like a bolt of lightning, and yet it was about a problem, no, more of a need, the need to avoid totally nailing the script, the need not to want to learn it, a whole mixture of things that I still haven't managed to unravel entirely.

Is that what he was criticising you for?

He was criticising me for not knowing my lines. It's true, I do sometimes skate on thin ice, but it's a rebellion, some sort of a fear of it becoming too automatic . . . I know that some actors do turn up knowing their script perfectly, especially when they've got a difficult scene to do. But for me, it's very hard to get it word-perfect. I can't seem to help leaving gaps, and I'm still not sure whether that's purely the fear of sounding too mechanical, or whether it's because I don't manage to make enough of a sustained effort to learn it perfectly. I feel the need to keep some kind of . . .

Space?

Yes. But that approach can play tricks on you, it's played tricks on me, anyway . . . I was totally mortified on that particular day. Really upset afterwards. I can remember it all, the set, the scene, the weather, everything. I thought it was unfair, because it seemed to me that I knew my lines well enough for us to rehearse and then start shooting. But, in actual fact, I think he was right. And you have to remember that André likes his actors very dynamic, he likes to use a lot of words, lots of dialogue, and he likes it very pacy . . .

He always uses a lot of 'dot, dot, dots' in his dialogues; you never see a full stop in a Téchiné screenplay ...

You're right, no full stops. He always wants to leave the possibility hanging that you're saying such and such but actually maybe that's not quite right, maybe the character would have said something else. And apparently, I'm a lot like that in real life, people have often told me so. It was the sound engineer on *Tom Thumb* who remarked on it, it made me laugh, I thought to myself, 'He's right, I often don't finish my sentences.'

We were starting to talk about Truffaut ... because in terms of important connections, your bond with Truffaut is clearly one of the most significant ... you did Mississippi Mermaid *with him ...*

Yes, and *The Last Metro.*

Mississippi Mermaid *was a commercial flop, whereas* The Last Metro *was a huge success.*

Yes.

The character in The Last Metro *was rather like you, she was a theatre director in love ...*

I remember that while Truffaut was writing it, he told me that he wanted to give me the role of a woman who bore a lot of responsibility. And after that, I was offered a lot of roles in the same mould, busy, not particularly appealing women, who often acted rather harshly, but women who worked like men, something which isn't very common even today. The problem is that whenever you

CLOSE UP AND PERSONAL

create male roles for women, the characters are, without fail, businesswomen. I remember the night of *The Last Metro* première, at a cinema which no longer exists, on the Champs-Elysées in Paris. At the end, people applauded, and then there was a very solemn drinks party where people came up to shake our hands, and I remember François kept saying, 'It's a funeral, it's a funeral, these are funereal condolences, it's a funeral.' He upset me so much that I came out of the screening in a terrible state and threw up in the Champs-Elysées flower beds. It was a success, but compliments can also seem like condolences in disguise . . . but you know, he always hated public occasions. He liked to communicate one-to-one, or by letter.

He didn't like high society . . .

No, not at all.

Perhaps he was even a little agoraphobic.

Yes, though I remember that he was sometimes very relaxed on set, and occasionally even managed some jokes when introducing a film. When we were introducing *The Last Metro* on the American festival circuit, I remember he used to love telling funny stories in English, because according to him that was something the Americans knew how to do better than us, so he put a lot of effort into making these amusing little speeches with a clever twist at the end . . .

He learnt that from Hitchcock.

Yes, absolutely.

Let's talk about Demy and The Umbrellas of Cherbourg
. . . you did at least three films with him.

Four actually: *The Umbrellas, The Young Girls of Rochefort, Once Upon a Time* and *A Slightly Pregnant Man.* I
received an invitation to the re-release of *Lola* with a
handwritten note from Jacques saying he very much
wanted to meet me. He told me afterwards that he'd seen
me in a rather mediocre film called *Ladies Man,* alongside
Danielle Darrieux and Mel Ferrer.

You've played Danielle Darrieux's daughter twice?

Yes.

The other time was in Scene of the Crime.

Actually three times. *Scene of the Crime* and *The Young
Girls.*

Oh yes, of course, The Young Girls *too.*

Yes, and then . . . a fourth time, because she's also my
mother in Ozon's *8 Women.*

Oh yes, that's true, of course.

It's like my relationship with Daniel Auteuil, whose sister
I played in a movie. I don't see Danielle Darrieux very
often, but when I do there's a real family bond, it's very
strange. I'm her film daughter.

Let's go back to Demy; it seems rather key.

Yes, because I was very young, and not at all sure that I wanted to continue doing movies. You see I'd started almost by accident, through my sister, when I played her sister in a film. As well as being shy, I wasn't very self-confident and meeting Jacques was a real turning point ... I was eighteen years old, he described a film that sounded totally original and daring, and I didn't hesitate ... the film took a long time to get off the ground, there were a lot of difficulties because I was pregnant, then I had my son, and we shot the film straight after my baby's birth. Yes, really. Two months later ...

Christian Vadim?

Yes. So it took a while before Mag Bodard[1] was able to get the film started, but it was one of those shoots that happen sometimes, you know, films where in spite of all the difficulties, everyone pulls together. And everything Jacques said to me at that time, while he was directing me, really broadened my mind. He broadened my mind and, at the same time, tore me apart. I'd never imagined that cinema could be like that, what kind of an experience filming and acting could be. I didn't have any idea of that yet.

And it must have been quite unusual technically?

Very. We had to learn all our lines from the pre-recorded score. And it was very, very complicated for him, because once he'd chosen the sets, he had to create the film in relation to the score, which had already been written and which therefore imposed its own rhythm.

1 The producer.

So playback was used for the whole film?

Yes, we acted the whole thing to a pre-recorded score. All of it. They used loudspeakers, even for the street scenes at night ... the music was recorded before the film, and I remember playing it to some friends while I was learning my part, and noticing how they were already completely bowled over ...

Michel Legrand ...

Yes, but also the words, because in this case, it really was both music and words.

Yes, yes.

Even before it existed it was an extremely moving concept.

And it was very successful ...

Yes.

Which placed you on a pedestal straight away. But at the same time, it was a completely original film.

It's an opera.

It's an art-house film.

Yes. It's a totally exceptional thing, an opera, a modern opera steeped in everyday life. Simultaneously real and poetic.

Exceptional for Demy as well – he never found that magic formula again.

You're thinking of *A Room in Town?*

Yes, which was an attempt to repeat the same formula.

It was a musical film, yes.

Much later.

Yes, much later.

And without Michel Legrand.

Yes.

But wasn't A Room in Town *also an old project?*

It was an idea he'd been thinking about for a while.

But he did do The Young Girls of Rochefort *a few years later, with your sister this time, and that became . . .*

A landmark film for French musical cinema, yes.

And was even adapted into a stage musical recently.

Yes. *The Umbrellas* was an opera because it was completely sung, whereas *The Young Girls* was more like an American musical.

Was that the first time you acted alongside your sister?

No, my first film with her was also my first proper film, *The Door Slams.*

Oh yes, The Door Slams. *So this was a reunion, but of course, this time you really were a sensational double-act . . .*

Oh yes, it was great. I think that to start with, it was a bit tricky for her because I'd already worked with Jacques Demy. She was worried that that would unbalance things, but after the first week, which was a little difficult . . .

Difficult?

Difficult because I knew him better, I'd already worked with him, and also it was summer and the film was physically challenging to shoot.

And this was a very different way of working, you recorded the songs first?

Yes, and we'd also worked on the choreography beforehand, in London and Paris . . . getting ready for the film together, learning our dance moves together, I must say that it . . . two sisters . . . even if you're very close, you don't usually spend all your time together – one is working in one place, the other somewhere else. Whereas this was an unexpected opportunity. I'm very glad that we experienced it, it was like when we were younger and used to live together . . .

It's a cult film now, but I think at the time it was less successful than The Umbrellas. *A special and long-lasting bond formed then between you and Jacques Demy . . .*

Yes, very long lasting, right until *A Room in Town*. Until we parted company over *A Room in Town*.

What was the disagreement about?

Jacques wanted to dub us, but Gérard Depardieu and I thought that our voices were too well known, fifteen years on from *The Umbrellas*. Seeing the actors' faces, with their own voices for the spoken words but other voices for the songs, would have been a lot less believable ... I was very firm about it, Jacques dug his heels in, so did I, so did Gérard. We worked with Michel Colombier, recorded some trial songs to prove that we could do it ... he wasn't at all convinced, which I can understand, and then, I don't know, I'm sure he thought we would give in, but we couldn't, so that was the end of it.

What about Michel Legrand?

I don't know what happened between Jacques and Michel. All I know is that he chose Colombier ... I don't think Michel Legrand was very enthused by the script. They didn't talk to each other for a long time, Jacques was such an uncompromising man, he bore a grudge. Luckily, we became friends again later. I used to meet up with him, right until he died. We even planned a great film together – he wanted to go to Russia and shoot *Anna Karenina* as a musical comedy.

The other filmmaker from your very early career is Roman Polanski, who'd just shot a film with your sister, Françoise Dorléac. No, I'm mistaken, Cul-de-Sac *was made just afterwards, wasn't it?*

Yes, a year and a half later.

So the film you made with him was Repulsion.

I met Roman while I was shooting *The Umbrellas.* He was in the area filming the credits for a composite film. One evening, he was filming on a boat, and I was with some friends who knew him. I found him completely fascinating, what an amazing character, such intense eyes, darting all over the place, incredibly alive. At that stage I'd never seen any of his films.

His first feature film, Knife in the Water, *hadn't come out yet.*

No. He contacted me in Paris soon afterwards, he'd seen *The Umbrellas* and loved it, and he asked me to do a film with him. I said, 'Sure, why not, of course,' and he gave me his adaptation of Roland Dubillard's *The Swallows* to read. And, like an idiot, at the time I thought it was a stupid role. I was annoyed and refused it. Then he offered me a film he'd written with Gérard Brach, in English for an American actress, it was called *Angel Face*, and ended up as *Repulsion*. I remember being close to Roman while we filmed it, and that the producer was one of his Polish friends, whose previous films were mostly rather hot B-movies.

Porn films?

I haven't seen them but I think so. Soft porn, maybe, but in any case, this was his first art-house film. So you had these two hedonist Poles in exile in England, Gérard Brach coming and going, and me, alone with the English crew ... on set, Roman almost always talked to me in French. I hardly speak in the film. I'm sure that my lines for the whole of *Repulsion* don't add up to more than five pages.

After The Umbrellas, *a 'Technicolor Musical', Repulsion was a black and white film.*

Yes. I find that, paradoxically, black and white tends to lend old films a somehow modern look, as if they've kept their integrity, whereas films in colour date much more quickly.

You haven't done many black and white films. There's the Rappeneau film, Gracious Living.

Yes. But black and white films are hardly ever made these days. I came in on the tail end. And today, I think that making a black and white film would be like committing professional hara-kiri.

And it would also seem affected.

That's down to television. TV shapes everything these days.

Weren't you freaked out by the role you played when you saw the film?

Absolutely not, I thought it was fantastic, I was very pleased. I remember Quincy Jones did the music, in London, and I went over to attend the recording sessions. And then it was a low-budget film, on a very small scale, and there was a fair amount of conflict, because the

English are very strict about their hours and he'd sometimes get angry when they would just down tools, right
in the middle of a take. We saw a lot of each other, talked
a lot, went to the movies together ... Life took us in
different directions, Roman isn't someone I see very
often, but I'm incredibly fond of him. It seems to me he's
had such a tragic life, and he's been blessed with amazing
strength to get him through it all ... and I'm not only
thinking of his wife's death, I'm thinking of it all: his
parents dying in the ghetto, the fact that he's not allowed
to work in or travel to the United States, that he's been
accused of rape, I think he's had an extremely difficult
life. But he's managed to overcome it all.

He's also got a lot of energy.

Yes. An unbelievable vital energy.

After Repulsion, *he decided to make a film with your sister.*

I was very happy for her to work with him. I wasn't
jealous of my sister and I didn't have time to be. I wonder
how things would have developed for the two of us.

*It's funny, because the twin-like quality that the two of you
had is filmic in itself ... the fact that Polanski made films
with you and with her, that Truffaut made films with her
and with you ...*

And Demy, when we really were pretty much twins.

Demy too, obviously. It's very striking.

Yes, I wonder how things would have ... I don't know,

because my sister was suffering a great deal at the time, she was very excessive, very radical, very wild and uncompromising.

Are you saying that she was the extrovert and you were the introvert?

Absolutely. In any case, that dichotomy is very noticeable when I look back over the interviews we did together for *The Young Girls*. But in fact it suited us. We complemented each other.

Filmography

1956

Les Collégiennes (*The Twilight Girls*), by André Hune-belle, with Estella Blain, Christine Carrère, Henri Guisol, Gaby Morlay, Elga Andersen, Agnès Laurent, Marie-Hélène Arnaud, Paul Guers, René Bergeron.

1960

Les portes claquent (*The Door Slams*), by Jacques Poitrenaud, with Françoise Dorléac, Michael Lonsdale, Jacqueline Maillan, Dany Saval, Noël Roquevert, Maurice Sarfati.

L'Homme à femmes (*Ladies Man*), by Jacques-Gérard Cornu, with Danielle Darrieux, Mel Ferrer, Claude Rich, Colette Fleury, Alan Scott, Pierre Brice, Nicolas Amato, Robert Rollys.

1961

Les Parisiennes – Ella – Antonia – Françoise – Sophie (*Beds and Broads*) (composite film), by Michel Boisrond and Claude Barma, with Johnny Hallyday, Dany Saval, Darry Cowl, Jean Poiret, Eddy Mitchell, Christian Marquand, Dany Robin, Françoise Brion, Françoise Arnoul.

1962

Et Satan conduit le bal (*And Satan Calls the Turns*), by Grisha Dabat, with Jacques Perrin, Françoise Brion,

Bernadette Lafont, Jacques Monod, Jacques Doniol-Valcroze.

Les Vacances portugaises (*Portuguese Vacation*), by Pierre Kast, with Françoise Arnoul, Michel Auclair, Jean-Pierre Aumont, Françoise Brion, Jean-Marc Bory, Pierre Vaneck, Daniel Gélin, Françoise Prévost, Edouard Molinaro.

Le Vice et la Vertu (*Vice and Virtue*), by Roger Vadim, adapted from the Sade, with Annie Girardot, Robert Hossein, Philippe Lemaire, Henri Virlojeux, Howard Vernon, Valéria Ciangottini, Luciana Paluzzi, O. E. Hasse, Georges Poujouly.

1963

Les Parapluies de Cherbourg (*The Umbrellas of Cherbourg*), by Jacques Demy, with Nino Castelnuovo, Anne Vernon, Marc Michel, Gisèle Grandpré, Ellen Farner, Mireille Perrey, Jean Champion (Palme d'Or, Cannes 1964).

Les Plus Belles Escroqueries du monde – L'Homme qui vendit la tour Eiffel – La Rivière de diamants – Les Cinq Bienfaiteurs de Fumiko – La Feuille de route (*World's Greatest Swindles*) (composite film), by Hiromichi Horikawa, Claude Chabrol and Roman Polanski, with Charles Denner, Jean-Pierre Cassel, Francis Blanche, Jean Seberg, Gérard Brach, Nicole Karen, Gabriella Giorgelli, Ken Mitsuda, Jan Teulings.

1964

La Chasse à l'homme (*The Gentle Art of Seduction*), by Edouard Molinaro, with Jean-Claude Brialy, Françoise Dorléac, Claude Rich, Jean-Paul Belmondo, Francis

Blanche, Bernard Blier, Micheline Presle, Michel Serrault, Marie Laforêt.

La Costanza delle ragione (*Avec amour et avec rage*), by Pasquale Festa Campanile, with Sami Frey.

Un monsieur de compagnie (*Male Companion*), by Philippe de Broca, with Jean-Claude Brialy, Annie Girardot, Jean-Pierre Cassel, Jean-Pierre Marielle, Rosy Varte, Sandra Milo, Marcel Dalio, Irma Demick, Valérie Lagrange.

1965

Le Chant du monde (*Song of the World*), by Marcel Camus, adapted from the Jean Giono, with Hardy Krüger, Charles Vanel, Marilu Tolo, Serge Marquand, Ginette Leclerc, Georgette Anys, Christian Mann, Michel Vitold.

Les Creatures (*The Creatures*), by Agnès Varda, with Michel Piccoli, Nicole Courcel, Jacques Charrier, Nino Castelnuovo, Eva Dahlbeck.

Das Liebeskarussell – Parade d'amour – Belles d'un jour – Belles d'un soir – Lolita – Who Wants to Sleep? (composite film), by Rolf Thiele and Alfred Weidenmann, with Curt Jürgens, Anita Ekberg, Gert Froebe, Heinz Rühmann, Nadja Tiller.

Répulsion (*Repulsion*), by Roman Polanski, with Yvonne Furneaux, Gérard Brach, Ian Hendry, John Fraser, Patrick Wymark.

La Vie de château (*Gracious Living*), by Jean-Paul Rappeneau, with Philippe Noiret, Henri Garcin, Pierre Brasseur, Mary Marquet (Prix Louis-Delluc 1965).

Les Petits Chats (*Wild Roots of Love*), by Jacques Villa, with Sylviane Margolle, Maïté Andrès, Ginette Pigeon, Pierre Dudan, Henri Nassiet, Geneviève Galea.

1966

Belle de Jour, by Luis Buñuel, adapted from the Joseph Kessel, with Michel Piccoli, Françoise Fabian, Pierre Clémenti, Francis Blanche, Bernard Fresson, Georges Marchal, Macha Méril, Jean Sorel, Geneviève Page (Golden Lion, Venice 1967).

Les Demoiselles de Rochefort (*The Young Girls of Rochefort*), by Jacques Demy, with Françoise Dorléac, Danielle Darrieux, George Chakiris, Jacques Perrin, Michel Piccoli, Gene Kelly, Henri Crémieux.

1967

Benjamin ou les mémoires d'un puceau (*The Diaries of an Innocent Boy*), by Michel Deville, with Michèle Morgan, Michel Piccoli, Pierre Clémenti, Catherine Rouvel, Jacques Dufilho, Odile Versois, Jean Lefebvre, Cécile Vassort, Alexandra Stewart (Prix Louis-Delluc 1967).

Manon 70, by Jean Aurel, adapted from the Abbé Prévost, with Sami Frey, Jean-Claude Brialy, Elsa Martinelli, Claude Génia, Paul Hubschmid.

Mayerling, by Terence Young, with Omar Sharif, Ava Gardner, James Mason, Lyne Chardonnet, Andréa Pansy, Geneviève Page, Moustache, Fiona Gélin, Howard Vernon.

1968

The April Fools, by Stuart Rosenberg, with Jack Lemmon, Charles Boyer, Sally Kellerman, Myrna Loy, Peter Lawford, Melinda Dillon, Jack Weston.

La Chamade (*Heartbeat*), by Alain Cavalier, adapted from the Françoise Sagan, with Michel Piccoli, Roger Van Hool, Amidou, Jacques Sereys, Irène Tunc.

La Sirène du Mississippi (*Mississippi Mermaid*), by François Truffaut, adapted from the William Irish, with Jean-Paul Belmondo, Michel Bouquet, Nelly Borgeaud, Marcel Berbert.

1969

Tout peut arriver (*Don't Be Blue*), by Philippe Labro, with Prudence Harrington, Jean-Claude Bouillon, Catherine Allégret, Chantal Goya, Fabrice Luchini.

Tristana, by Luis Buñuel, with Fernando Rey, Franco Nero, Lola Gaos, Jesús Fernández, Antonio Casas, Sergio Mendizábal, José Calvo.

1970

Peau d'Âne (*Once Upon a Time*), by Jacques Demy, adapted from the Charles Perrault, with Jean Marais, Micheline Presle, Jacques Perrin, Delphine Seyrig, Fernand Ledoux, Henri Crémieux, Sacha Pitoëff, Pierre Repp, Myriam Boyer.

1971

Liza (*Love to Eternity*), by Marco Ferreri, adapted from the Ennio Flaiano, with Marcello Mastroianni, Corinne Marchand, Michel Piccoli, Valérie Stroh, Pascal Laperrousaz.

Ça n'arrive qu'aux autres (*It Only Happens to Others*), by Nadine Trintignant, with Marcello Mastroianni, Dominique Labourier, Catherine Allégret, Marie Trintignant, Danièle Lebrun, Serge Marquand, Catherine Hiegel.

Un flic (*Dirty Money*), by Jean-Pierre Melville, with Alain Delon, Paul Crauchet, Richard Crenna, Simone Valère, André Pousse, Jean Desailly, Ricardo Cucciolla.

1973

L'Événement le plus important depuis que l'homme a marché sur la Lune (*A Slightly Pregnant Man*), by Jacques Demy, with Marcello Mastroianni, Myriam Boyer, Micheline Presle, Alice Sapritch, Micheline Dax, Jacques Legras, Maurice Biraud, Tonie Marshall, Claude Melki.

Touche pas à la femme blanche (*Don't Touch the White Woman!*), by Marco Ferreri, with Philippe Noiret, Michel Piccoli, Serge Reggiani, Ugo Tognazzi, Marcello Mastroianni, Alain Cuny, Darry Cowl.

1974

L'Agression (*Act of Aggression*), by Gérard Pirès, with Jean-Louis Trintignant, Claude Brasseur, Robert Charlebois, Daniel Auteuil, Valérie Mairesse, Daniel Duval, Philippe Brigaud, Michèle Grellier, Franco Fabrizi.

Fatti di gente per bene (*Drama of the Rich*), by Mauro Bolognini, with Giancarlo Giannini, Fernando Rey, Marcel Bozzuffi, Laura Betti, Tina Aumont, Paolo Bonacelli.

La Femme aux bottes rouges (*The Woman with Red Boots*),

by Luis Buñuel, with Fernando Rey, Jacques Weber, Laura Betti.

Hustle, by Robert Aldrich, with Burt Reynolds, Eddie Albert, Ernest Borgnine, Don Barry, Ben Johnson, Paul Winfield, Eileen Brennan, Robert Englund.

Zig-zig (*Zig-Zag*), by Laszlo Szabo, with Bernadette Lafont, Jean-Pierre Kalfon, Georgette Anys, Walter Chiari, Hubert Deschamps, Yves Afonso.

1975

Le Sauvage (*Call me Savage*), by Jean-Paul Rappeneau, with Yves Montand, Tony Roberts, Luigi Vannucchi, Dana Wynter.

1976

Anima persa (*Lost Soul*), by Dino Risi, with Vittorio Gassman, Anicée Alvina, Danilo Mattei.

March or Die, by Dick Richards, with Gene Hackman, Terence Hill, Marcel Bozzuffi, Max Von Sydow, Jean Rougerie, Rufus, Ian Holm, Jack O'Halloran, Jean Champion.

Si c'était à refaire (*Second Chance*), by Claude Lelouch, with Anouk Aimée, Niels Arestrup, Charles Denner, Francis Huster, Zoé Chauveau, Bernard-Pierre Donnadieu, Jean-Pierre Kalfon, Jacques Villeret, Jean-Jacques Briot.

1977

Écoute voir (*See Here My Love*), by Hugo Santiago, with Sami Frey, Anne Parillaud, Didier Haudepin,

Jean-François Stévenin, François Dyrek, Florence Delay, Antoine Vitez.

II casotto (*Beach House*), by Sergio Citti, with Jodie Foster, Ugo Tognazzi, Michèle Placido, Marie-Angela Melato, Luigi Proietti, Paolo Stoppa.

1978

L'Argent des autres (*Other People's Money*), by Christian de Chalonge, with Jean-Louis Trintignant, Claude Brasseur, Michel Serrault, François Perrot, Juliet Berto, Umberto Orsini, Francis Lemaire, Raymond Bussières, Michel Berto.

Ils sont grands ces petits (*These Kids are Grown-Ups*), by Joël Santoni, with Claude Brasseur, Claude Piéplu, Jean-François Balmer, Eva Darlan, Yves Robert, Roland Blanche, Jean-Pierre Coffe, Michel Berto.

1979

A nous deux (*Us Two*), by Claude Lelouch, with Jacques Dutronc, Jacques Villeret, Daniel Auteuil, Richard Bohringer, Paul Préboist, Bernard Lecoq, Xavier Saint-Macary, Anne Jousset, Myriam Mézières.

Courage fuyons (*Courage – Let's Run*), by Yves Robert, with Jean Rochefort, Philippe Leroy-Beaulieu, Michel Beaune, Dominique Lavanant, Michel Aumont, Christophe Bourseiller, Gérard Darmon, Robert Webber, Christian Charmetant.

1980

Le Dernier Métro (*The Last Metro*), by François Truffaut, with Gérard Depardieu, Maurice Risch, Richard Bohringer, Sabine Haudepin, Andréa Ferréol, Jean Poiret, Paulette Dubost, Heinz Bennent, Jean-Louis Richard (Best Actress, Cesar 1981).

Je vous aime (*I Love You All*), by Claude Berri, with Alain Souchon, Serge Gainsbourg, Gérard Depardieu, Jean-Louis Trintignant, Ysabelle Lacamp, Christian Marquand, Thomas Langmann, Dominique Besnehard.

Reporters (documentary), by Raymond Depardon, with Richard Gere, Coluche, Mireille Darc, Alain Delon, Serge Gainsbourg, Jean-Luc Godard, Gene Kelly, Max Meynier, Mireille Mathieu.

1981

Le Choc (*Shock*), by Robin Davis, with Alain Delon, Stéphane Audran, Étienne Chicot, Philippe Léotard, Catherine Leprince, François Perrot, Féodor Atkine, Jean-Louis Richard, Alexandra Stewart.

Le Choix des armes (*Choice of Arms*), by Alain Corneau, with Yves Montand, Gérard Depardieu, Gérard Lanvin, Michel Galabru, Marc Chapiteau, Christian Marquand, Jean Rougerie, Jean-Claude Dauphin, Richard Anconina.

Hôtel des Amériques (*Hotel America*), by André Téchiné, with Patrick Dewaere, Étienne Chicot, Sabine Haudepin, Josiane Balasko, François Perrot, Dominique Lavanant, Jacques Nolot.

1982

L'Africain (*The African*), by Philippe de Broca, with Philippe Noiret, Jean-François Balmer, Jacques François,

Jean Benguigui, Gérard Brach, Joseph Momo, Vivian Reed, Raymond Aquilon.

The Hunger, by Tony Scott, with David Bowie, Susan Sarandon, Willem Dafoe, Cliff de Young, Beth Ehlers, Dan Hedaya, Bessie Love.

1983

Le Bon Plaisir, by Francis Girod, adapted from the Françoise Giroud, with Jean-Louis Trintignant, Michel Serrault, Michel Auclair, Hippolyte Girardot, Alexandra Stewart, Janine Darcey, Jacques Sereys, Christine Ockrent, Laurence Masliah.

Fort Saganne, by Alain Corneau, with Gérard Depardieu, Sophie Marceau, Philippe Noiret, Michel Duchaussoy, Robin Renucci, Pierre Tornade, Roger Dumas, Florent Pagny, Hippolyte Girardot.

1984

Paroles et Musique (*Love Songs*), by Élie Chouraqui, with Christopher Lambert, Richard Anconina, Jacques Perrin, Dayle Haddon, Dominique Lavanant, Charlotte Gainsbourg, Laszlo Szabo, Clémentine Célarié.

1985

Le Lieu du crime (*Scene of the Crime*), by André Téchiné, with Wadeck Stanczak, Claire Nebout, Danielle Darrieux, Victor Lanoux, Jean-Claude Adelin, Nicolas Giraudi, Jacques Nolot.

Speriamo che sia femina (*Let's Hope It's a Girl*) by Mario Monicelli, with Liv Ullmann, Bernard Blier, Philippe

Noiret, Stefania Sandrelli, Lucrezia Lante Della Rovere, Giuliana de Sio, Giuliano Gemma.

1987

Agent trouble (*The Man Who Loved Zoos*), by Jean-Pierre Mocky, with Richard Bohringer, Tom Novembre, Dominique Lavanant, Pierre Arditi, Sylvie Joly, Kristin Scott-Thomas, Dominique Zardi, Elisabeth Vitali, Maurice Le Roux.

Fréquence meurtre (*Frequent Death*), by Elisabeth Rappeneau, with André Dussolier, Martin Lamotte, Étienne Chicot, Madeleine Marie.

1988

Drôle d'endroit pour une rencontre (*Strange Place for an Encounter*), by François Dupeyron, with Gérard Depardieu, Nathalie Cardone, Jean-Pierre Sentier, André Wilms.

Helmut Newton: Frames from the Edge (documentary), by Adrian Maben, with Sigourney Weaver, Charlotte Rampling, Faye Dunaway, Capucine.

1990

La Reine blanche, by Jean-Loup Hubert, with Richard Bohringer, Bernard Giraudeau, Jean Carmet, Marie Bunel, Isabelle Carré, Geneviève Fontanel.

1991

Contre l'oubli (documentary), by Chantal Akerman, with Philippe Noiret, Jane Birkin, Bertrand Blier, Anouk

Grinberg, Alain Corneau, Alain Souchon, Raymond Depardon, Sami Frey.

Indochine, by Régis Wargnier, with Linh Dan Phan, Vincent Perez, Jean Yanne, Dominique Blanc, Henri Marteau, Andrzej Seweryn, Hubert Saint-Macary.

1992

Les Demoiselles ont eu vingt-cinq ans (documentary), by Agnès Varda, with Jacques Perrin.

Ma saison préférée (*My Favourite Season*), by André Téchiné, with Daniel Auteuil, Jean-Pierre Bouvier, Marthe Villalonga, Chiara Mastroianni, Anthony Prada, Carmen Chaplin, Roschdy Zem, Bruno Todeschini, Ingrid Caven.

1993

La Partie d'échecs (*The Chess Game*), by Yves Hanchar, with Pierre Richard, Denis Lavant, James Wilby, Delphine Bibet.

1994

Les Cent et Une Nuits (*A Hundred and One Nights*), by Agnès Varda, with Michel Piccoli, Marcello Mastroianni, Mathieu Demy, Emmanuel Salinger, Henri Garcin, Robert de Niro, Gérard Depardieu, Alain Delon, Jean-Paul Belmondo.

Le Couvent (*The Convent*), by Manoel de Oliveira, with John Malkovich, Luis Miguel Cintra, Leonor Silveira.

Court toujours: L'Inconnu (short TV film), by lsmaël Ferroukhi, with Predrag-Miki Manojlovic.

1995

Les Voleurs (*Thieves*), by André Téchiné, with Daniel Auteuil, Laurence Côte, Benoît Magimel, Didier Bezace, Fabienne Babe, Julien Rivière, Chiara Mastroianni.

1996

Généalogies d'un crime (*Genealogies of a Crime*), by Raúl Ruiz, with Michel Piccoli, Melvil Poupaud, Bernadette Lafont, Monique Mélinand, Jean-Yves Gautier, Mathieu Amalric, Hubert Saint-Macary, Jean Badin, Andrzej Seweryn.

1997

Place Vendôme, by Nicole Garcia, with Jean-Pierre Bacri, Emmanuelle Seigner, Jacques Dutronc, Bernard Fresson, François Berléand, Laszlo Szabo, Philippe Clévenot.

Pola X, by Leos Carax, with Guillaume Depardieu, Katherina Golubeva, Delphine Chuillot, Anne Brochet, Patachou.

1998

Belle Maman (*Beautiful Mother*), by Gabriel Aghion, with Vincent Lindon, Mathilde Seigner, Line Renaud, Danièle Lebrun, Jean Yanne, Stéphane Audran.

Est–Ouest (*East–West*), by Régis Wargnier, with Sandrine Bonnaire, Oleg Menchikov, Hubert Saint-Macary, Ruben Tapiero, Sergueï Bodrov, René Féret.

Le Temps retrouvé (*Time Regained*), by Raúl Ruiz, with Marcello Mazzarella, Vincent Perez, Mathilde Seigner, Chiara Mastroianni, Marie-France Pisier, John

Malkovich, Pascal Greggory, Christian Vadim, Emmanuelle Béart.

Le Vent de la nuit (*Night Wind*), by Philippe Garrel, with Xavier Beauvois, Daniel Duval, Jacques Lassalle, Marie Vialle, Anita Blond.

1999

Dancer in the Dark, by Lars von Trier, with Björk, David Morse, Peter Stormare, Jean-Marc Barr (Palme d'Or, Cannes 2000).

2000

Absolument fabuleux (*Absolutely Fabulous*), by Gabriel Aghion, with Josiane Balasko, Nathalie Baye, Marie Gillain, Vincent Elbaz, Claude Gensac, Yves Rénier, Saïd Taghmaoui, Chantal Goya, Stéphane Bern.

Je rentre à la maison (*I Go Home*), by Manoel de Oliveira, with Michel Piccoli, John Malkovich, Antoine Chappey, Sylvie Testud, Adrien de Van.

The Musketeer, by Peter Hyams, with Stephen Rea, Tim Roth, Justin Chambers, Jean-Pierre Castaldi, Mena Suvari, Tsilla Chelton, Daniel Mesguich.

Le Petit Poucet (*Tom Thumb*), by Olivier Dahan, adapted from the Charles Perrault, with Nils Hugon, Romane Bohringer, Pierre Berriau, Élodie Bouchez, Romain Duris, Samy Nacéri, Saïd Taghmaoui, Benoît Magimel, Dominique Hulin.

2001

Au plus près du paradis (*Nearest to Heaven*), by Tonie

Marshall, with William Hurt, Hélène Fillières, Patrice Chéreau, Emmanuelle Devos, Bernard Lecoq, Nathalie Richard, Gilbert Melki, Paulina Porizkova.

Huit femmes (*8 Women*), by François Ozon, with Isabelle Huppert, Emmanuelle Béart, Fanny Ardant, Virginie Ledoyen, Danielle Darrieux, Ludivine Sagnier, Firmine Richard.

Les Liaisons dangereuses (*Dangerous Liaisons*) (TV series), by Josée Dayan, with Rupert Everett, Nastassja Kinski, Leelee Sobieski, Danielle Darrieux.

Nuages: Lettres à mon fils (documentary), by Marion Hänsel, with Charlotte Rampling, Barbara Auer, Antje De Boeck.

2002

Un filme falado (*A Talking Picture*), by Manoel de Oliveira, with Leonor Silveira, John Malkovich, Stefania Sandrelli, Irène Papas.

2003

Princesse Marie (*Princess Marie*) (TV film), by Benoît Jacquot, with Heinz Bennent, Anne Bennent, Isild Le Besco, Elisabeth Orth, Gertraud Jesserer, Christoph Moosbrugger, Dominique Reymond, Didier Flamand, Edith Perret, Christian Vadim.

The dates shown correspond to the year the film was made.

INDEX